TAPESTRY

Reading 1

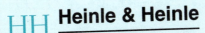

Virginia L. Guleff

M. E. Sokolik

Carolyn Lowther

Heinle & Heinle

Thomson Learning™

Australia • Canada • Denmark • Japan • Mexico
New Zealand • Philippines • Puerto Rico • Singapore
Spain • United Kingdom • United States

I'd like to thank my husband Michael Guleff for his patience and support during the completion of this project.

Developmental Editors: Jennifer Monaghan, Jill Korey O'Sullivan
Sr. Production Coordinator: Maryellen E. Killeen
Market Development Director: Charlotte Sturdy
Sr. Manufacturing Coordinator: Mary Beth Hennebury
Interior Design: Julia Gecha
Illustrations: Pre-Press Company, Inc.,
  Anthony Accardo

Photo Research: Martha Friedman
Cover Design: Ha Nguyen Design
Cover Images: PhotoDisc®
Composition/Production: Pre-Press Company, Inc.
Freelance Production Editor: Janet McCartney
Copyeditor: Timothy Lemire
Printer/Binder: Bawden

For permission to use material from this text, contact us:
web   www.thomsonrights.com
fax   1-800-730-2215
phone   1-800-730-2214

For photo credits, see page 198.

Heinle & Heinle Publishers
20 Park Plaza
Boston, MA 02116

UK/EUROPE/MIDDLE EAST:
Thomson Learning
Berkshire House
168-173 High Holborn
London, WC1V 7AA, United Kingdom

AUSTRALIA/NEW ZEALAND:
Nelson/Thomson Learning
102 Dodds Street
South Melbourne
Victoria 3205 Australia

CANADA:
Nelson/Thomson Learning
1120 Birchmount Road
Scarborough, Ontario
Canada M1K 5G4

LATIN AMERICA:
Thomson Learning
Seneca, 53
Colonia Polanco
11560 México D.F. México

ASIA (excluding Japan):
Thomson Learning
60 Albert Street #15-01
Albert Complex
Singapore 189969

JAPAN:
Thomson Learning
Palaceside Building, 5F
1-1-1 Hitotsubashi, Chiyoda-ku
Tokyo 100 0003, Japan

SPAIN:
Thomson Learning
Calle Magallanes, 25
28015-Madrid
España

Library of Congress Cataloging-in-Publication Data
Guleff, Virginia L.
  Tapestry reading 1 / Virginia L. Guleff, M. E. Sokolik, Carolyn Lowther.
    p. cm.
  ISBN 0-8384-0568-1 (alk. paper)
    1. English language—Textbooks for foreign speakers. 2. Reading comprehension—Problems, exercises, etc.
3. College readers. I. Title: Tapestry reading one. II. Sokolik, M. E. (Margaret E.) III. Lowther, Carolyn IV. Title.

PE1128 .G85 2000
428.6'4—dc21

99-057630

 This book is printed on acid-free recycled paper.

Printed in the United States of America.
1 2 3 4 5 6 7 8 9 03 02 01 00 99

A VERY SPECIAL THANK YOU

The publisher and authors would like to thank the following coordinators and instructors who have offered many helpful insights and suggestions for change throughout the development of the new *Tapestry*.

Alicia Aguirre, *Cañada College*
Fred Allen, *Mission College*
Maya Alvarez-Galvan, *University of Southern California*
Geraldine Arbach, *Collège de l'Outaouais, Canada*
Dolores Avila, *Pasadena City College*
Sarah Bain, *Eastern Washington University*
Kate Baldus, *San Francisco State University*
Fe Baran, *Chabot College*
Gail Barta, *West Valley College*
Karen Bauman, *Biola University*
Liza Becker, *Mt. San Antonio College*
Leslie Biaggi, *Miami-Dade Community College*
Andrzej Bojarczak, *Pasadena City College*
Nancy Boyer, *Golden West College*
Glenda Bro, *Mt. San Antonio College*
Brooke Brummitt, *Palomar College*
Linda Caputo, *California State University, Fresno*
Alyce Campbell, *Mt. San Antonio College*
Barbara Campbell, *State University of New York, Buffalo*
Robin Carlson, *Cañada College*
Ellen Clegg, *Chapman College*
Karin Cintron, *Aspect ILS*
Diane Colvin, *Orange Coast College*
Martha Compton, *University of California, Irvine*
Nora Dawkins, *Miami-Dade Community College*
Beth Erickson, *University of California, Davis*
Charles Estus, *Eastern Michigan University*
Gail Feinstein Forman, *San Diego City College*
Jeffra Flaitz, *University of South Florida*
Kathleen Flynn, *Glendale Community College*
Ann Fontanella, *City College of San Francisco*
Sally Gearhart, *Santa Rosa Junior College*
Alice Gosak, *San José City College*
Kristina Grey, *Northern Virginia Community College*
Tammy Guy, *University of Washington*
Gail Hamilton, *Hunter College*
Patty Heiser, *University of Washington*
Virginia Heringer, *Pasadena City College*

Catherine Hirsch, *Mt. San Antonio College*
Helen Huntley, *West Virginia University*
Nina Ito, *California State University, Long Beach*
Patricia Jody, *University of South Florida*
Diana Jones, *Angloamericano, Mexico*
Loretta Joseph, *Irvine Valley College*
Christine Kawamura, *California State University, Long Beach*
Gregory Keech, *City College of San Francisco*
Kathleen Keesler, *Orange Coast College*
Daryl Kinney, *Los Angeles City College*
Maria Lerma, *Orange Coast College*
Mary March, *San José State University*
Heather McIntosh, *University of British Columbia, Canada*
Myra Medina, *Miami-Dade Community College*
Elizabeth Mejia, *Washington State University*
Cristi Mitchell, *Miami-Dade Community College*
Sylvette Morin, *Orange Coast College*
Blanca Moss, *El Paso Community College*
Karen O'Neill, *San José State University*
Bjarne Nielsen, *Central Piedmont Community College*
Katy Ordon, *Mission College*
Luis Quesada, *Miami-Dade Community College*
Gustavo Ramírez Toledo, *Colegio Cristóbol Colón, Mexico*
Nuha Salibi, *Orange Coast College*
Alice Savage, *North Harris College*
Dawn Schmid, *California State University, San Marcos*
Mary Kay Seales, *University of Washington*
Denise Selleck, *City College of San Francisco*
Gail Slater, *Brooklyn and Staten Island Superintendency*
Susanne Spangler, *East Los Angeles College*
Karen Stanley, *Central Piedmont Community College*
Sara Storm, *Orange Coast College*
Margaret Teske, *ELS Language Centers*
Maria Vargas-O'Neel, *Miami-Dade Community College*
James Wilson, *Mt. San Antonio College and Pasadena City College*
Karen Yoshihara, *Foothill College*

ACKNOWLEDGMENTS

Thanks to Erik Rogers for his assistance in developing the instructor's manual and for his insightful comments on the discussion questions. Thanks also to Jill Kinkade for her help with the CNN video. I would especially like to thank Erik Gundersen for his capable and thoughtful guidance throughout the development of this series. Finally, and most importantly, love and thanks to Jim Duber for his support and help throughout this writing/editing process.

Tapestry Reading 1: Contents

CHAPTER	READING SKILLS FOCUS	LANGUAGE LEARNING STRATEGIES
1 College Life: Difficult Dreams Page 2	Using an English dictionary Previewing your reading Making a reading notebook Keeping a Vocabulary Log	Preview your reading to understand it better. Use an English dictionary to learn more about English words
2 Water: Our Most Important Resource Page 24	Scanning for information Understanding implied ideas Keeping a reading journal	Scan to find information quickly. Understand implied ideas in your reading.
3 Healthy Habits Page 42	Finding examples in your reading Skimming to get the main idea	Find examples to understand important ideas in your reading. Skim a reading to understand the main idea.
4 Only One Earth Page 60	Using background knowledge Finding topic sentences	Use your background knowledge to help you understand a reading. Find the topic sentences of paragraphs to understand the main ideas.
5 Trains, Planes, and Automobiles Page 80	Using a graphic organizer Making a time line	Use a graphic organizer to help you organize information. Make a time line to help you understand events in your reading.

ACADEMIC POWER STRATEGIES	CNN VIDEO CLIPS	READING OPPORTUNITIES
Make a study plan to become a better student.	"ESL School" A school in California has a program for children and their parents to study English together.	Reading 1: a story about a young man who achieves his academic dream, despite a difficult life Reading 2: a newspaper article about the rules of a college classroom Reading 3: a transcript from a radio report about the importance of education in the current job market
Keep a reading journal to think about your ideas and your learning.	"Water and Cancer" A look at drinking water in the United States—where it comes from and how safe it is.	Reading 1: a chart that gives information about how much water different things need Reading 2: an article about the safety of drinking water Reading 3: an article about the uses of reclaimed water
Set realistic academic goals.	"Stress Depression" An explanation of what causes job stress in women and how stress affects women's and men's health differently.	Reading 1: an article about an Olympic athlete who suffers from asthma Reading 2: a magazine article about home remedies Reading 3: a book excerpt about caffeine
Practice what you learn to connect your reading with your life.	"Garbage School" A landfill provides heat to a nearby high school.	Reading 1: an article about the environmental dangers of overfishing Reading 2: an article about the work of a fur trapper Reading 3: an article about the concern over the extinction of many plants and animal species Reading 4: an article about the largest garbage dump in the Middle East
Study in a group to better understand information from your classes.	"Subway Etiquette" New Yorkers get training on how to be polite on public transportation.	Reading 1: an article about a free public bicycle program in San Francisco Reading 2: an article about high-speed trains Reading 3: an article about electric cars Reading 4: an article about the Wright brothers, the inventors of the first airplane

CHAPTER	READING SKILLS FOCUS	LANGUAGE LEARNING STRATEGIES

ACADEMIC POWER STRATEGIES	**CNN VIDEO CLIPS**	**READING OPPORTUNITIES**
Avoid distractions when you study.	"Fast Food" Finding healthier alternatives to fast food when you don't have a lot of time to cook.	Reading 1: an article about fast food restaurants in Jamaica Reading 2: an article about the first McDonald's restaurant Reading 3: an article about ordering takeout and delivery food over the Internet Reading 4: an article about a new kind of fast food restaurant in Singapore
Organize your personal study space to improve your study sessions.	"Marriage & Family Therapists" For some families, therapists can make life at home much better.	Reading 1: an article about a controversial African wedding tradition Reading 2: an article about a modern dowry given to a bride in China Reading 3: an article about a traditional Cretan style of love song Reading 4: an article about the origins of some Jewish wedding traditions
Understand your school's rules about plagiarism.	"Totem Poles" An explanation of the role of totem poles in Native American traditions.	Reading 1: an article about myths and mythology Reading 2: a Native American folktale about the creation of a particular kind of fish Reading 3: a Japanese myth about a magic crane Reading 4: a Nigerian myth about humility Reading 5: a Greek myth about a man's dangerous journey to the underworld
Plan enough time to complete your assignments.	"Internet Shopping" A look at a new trend in shopping—Internet malls.	Reading 1: an article about a Vietnamese shopping mall in Texas Reading 2: an article examining whether shopping malls should be considered public or private places Reading 3: an article about the quality of customer service in the United States Reading 4: an article about ordering groceries over the Internet
Find and use campus resources when you need help with your classes.	"The CIA and UFOs" The CIA questions the Air Force's explanations for unidentified flying objects.	Reading 1: an excerpt from a web site about the selection and training of astronauts in the United States Reading 2: a magazine article about the discovery of a new planet Reading 3: an article about the Hale-Bopp comet Reading 4: an article about a scientific organization that searches for life on other planets

Welcome to TAPESTRY!

Empower your students with the Tapestry Reading series!

Language learning can be seen as an ever-developing tapestry woven with many threads and colors. The elements of the tapestry are related to different language skills such as listening and speaking, reading, and writing; the characteristics of the teachers; the desires, needs, and backgrounds of the students; and the general second language development process. When all of these elements are working together harmoniously, the result is a colorful, continuously growing tapestry of language competence of which the student and the teacher can be proud.

Tapestry is built upon a framework of concepts that helps students become proficient in English and prepared for the academic and social challenges in college and beyond. The following principles underlie the instruction provided in all of the components of the **Tapestry** program:

- ◆ Empowering students to be responsible for their learning
- ◆ Using Language Learning Strategies and Academic Power Strategies to enhance one's learning, both in and out of the classroom
- ◆ Offering motivating activities that recognize a variety of learning styles
- ◆ Providing authentic and meaningful input to heighten learning and communication
- ◆ Learning to understand and value different cultures
- ◆ Integrating language skills to increase communicative competence
- ◆ Providing goals and ongoing self-assessment to monitor progress

Guide to Tapestry Reading

Setting Goals focuses students' attention on the learning they will do in each chapter.

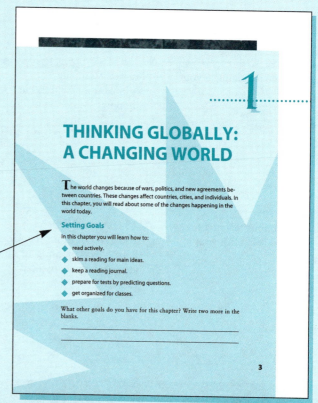

1

THINKING GLOBALLY: A CHANGING WORLD

The world changes because of wars, politics, and new agreements between countries. These changes affect countries, cities, and individuals. In this chapter, you will read about some of the changes happening in the world today.

Setting Goals

In this chapter you will learn how to:

- ◆ read actively.
- ◆ skim a reading for main ideas.
- ◆ keep a reading journal.
- ◆ prepare for tests by predicting questions.
- ◆ get organized for classes.

What other goals do you have for this chapter? Write two more in the blanks.

_____

_____

3

Stimulating reading selections from articles, stories, poems, interviews, essays, book excerpts, and more prepare students to read and comprehend a variety of academic texts.

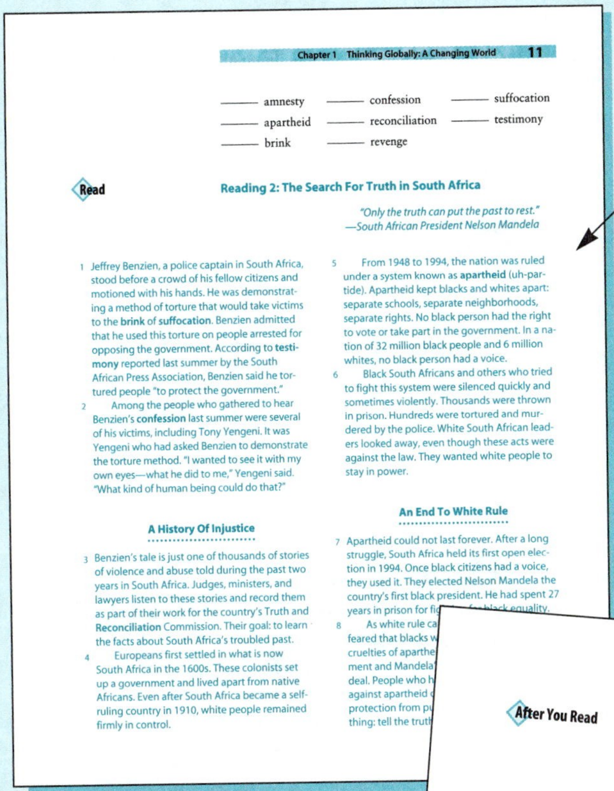

Language Learning Strategies help students maximize their learning and become proficient in English.

Apply the Strategy activities encourage students to take charge of their learning and immediately use their new skills and strategies.

First page (page 11)

—— amnesty   —— confession   —— suffocation

—— apartheid   —— reconciliation   —— testimony

—— brink   —— revenge

Read

Reading 2: The Search For Truth in South Africa

"Only the truth can put the past to rest."
—South African President Nelson Mandela

1 Jeffrey Benzien, a police captain in South Africa, stood before a crowd of his fellow citizens and motioned with his hands. He was demonstrating a method of torture that would take victims to the **brink** of **suffocation**. Benzien admitted that he used this torture on people arrested for opposing the government. According to **testimony** reported last summer by the South African Press Association, Benzien said he tortured people "to protect the government."

2 Among the people who gathered to hear Benzien's **confession** last summer were several of his victims, including Tony Yengeni. It was Yengeni who had asked Benzien to demonstrate the torture method. "I wanted to see it with my own eyes—what he did to me," Yengeni said. "What kind of human being could do that?"

A History Of Injustice

3 Benzien's tale is just one of thousands of stories of violence and abuse told during the past two years in South Africa. Judges, ministers, and lawyers listen to these stories and record them as part of their work for the country's Truth and **Reconciliation** Commission. Their goal: to learn the facts about South Africa's troubled past.

4 Europeans first settled in what is now South Africa in the 1600s. These colonists set up a government and lived apart from native Africans. Even after South Africa became a self-ruling country in 1910, white people remained firmly in control.

5 From 1948 to 1994, the nation was ruled under a system known as **apartheid** (uh-par-tide). Apartheid kept blacks and whites apart: separate schools, separate neighborhoods, separate rights. No black person had the right to vote or take part in the government. In a nation of 32 million black people and 6 million whites, no black person had a voice.

6 Black South Africans and others who tried to fight this system were silenced quickly and sometimes violently. Thousands were thrown in prison. Hundreds were tortured and murdered by the police. White South African leaders looked away, even though these acts were against the law. They wanted white people to stay in power.

An End To White Rule

7 Apartheid could not last forever. After a long struggle, South Africa held its first open election in 1994. Once black citizens had a voice, they used it. They elected Nelson Mandela the country's first black president. He had spent 27 years in prison for fighting for black equality.

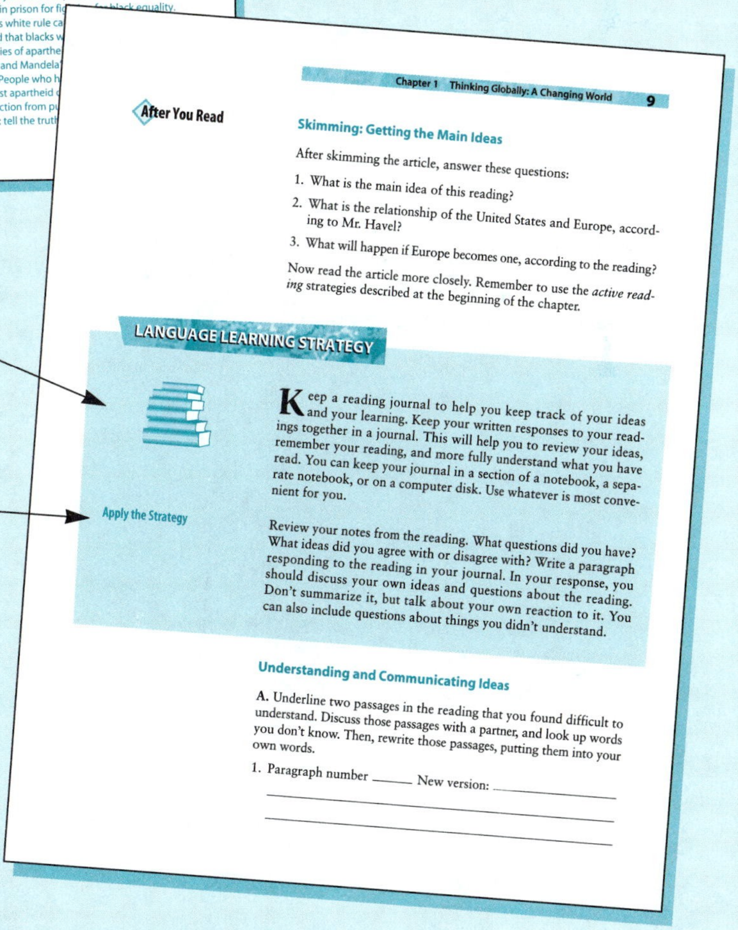

8 As white rule ca— feared that blacks w— cruelties of aparthe— ment and Mandela— deal. People who h— against apartheid — protection from p— thing: tell the trut—

Second page (page 9)

After You Read

Skimming: Getting the Main Ideas

After skimming the article, answer these questions:

1. What is the main idea of this reading?
2. What is the relationship of the United States and Europe, according to Mr. Havel?
3. What will happen if Europe becomes one, according to the reading?

Now read the article more closely. Remember to use the *active reading* strategies described at the beginning of the chapter.

LANGUAGE LEARNING STRATEGY

Apply the Strategy

Keep a reading journal to help you keep track of your ideas and your learning. Keep your written responses to your readings together in a journal. This will help you to review your ideas, remember your reading, and more fully understand what you have read. You can keep your journal in a section of a notebook, a separate notebook, or on a computer disk. Use whatever is most convenient for you.

Review your notes from the reading. What questions did you have? What ideas did you agree with or disagree with? Write a paragraph responding to the reading in your journal. In your response, you should discuss your own ideas and questions about the reading. Don't summarize it, but talk about your own reaction to it. You can also include questions about things you didn't understand.

Understanding and Communicating Ideas

A. Underline two passages in the reading that you found difficult to understand. Discuss those passages with a partner, and look up words you don't know. Then, rewrite those passages, putting them into your own words.

1. Paragraph number _____ New version: _____
   _____
   _____

Tapestry Threads provide students with interesting facts and quotes that jumpstart classroom discussions.

CNN® video clips provide authentic input and expand the readings to further develop language skills.

Academic Power Strategies give students the knowledge and skills to become successful, independent learners.

Getting Started

This chapter looks at food and dietary habits. Read these titles:

- "Do You Eat Smart?" a quiz from the *Los Angeles Times*
- "America Weighs In," a research article by Shannon Dortch
- "A Pyramid of Health," an article by Daniel Rogov

> **What is food to one man may be fierce poison to others.**
> —LUCRETIUS (95–55 B.C.E.), *DE RARUM NATURA*

1. Based on these titles, predict the ideas this chapter will cover. List them here. _____
_____
_____

2. What do you already know about healthy eating? _____
_____

3. What kind of diet does your home country have? _____
_____

4. Look ahead at the pictures and charts in this chapter. What do these tell you about the topic of the chapter? _____
_____

5. What do you want to learn from this chapter? Write down two questions you have about food and diet. _____
_____
_____

TUNING IN: "Istanbul Dining"

© CNN

Watch the CNN video about Istanbul dining. Discuss these questions with your class:

- What kinds of food are served in Istanbul?
- Describe what mealtimes are like in Istanbul.
- How does the Turkish style of eating compare with the style of eating in your native culture?

ACADEMIC POWER STRATEGY

Read newspapers and magazines to stay informed about current issues and arguments. Many students find they don't have enough time to keep up with current events. They stop reading newspapers and magazines when they go to college because they have so much reading to do for their courses. However, reading about current events can help you in your course work.

- Many problems in courses such as history, sociology, or psychology, have direct connections to current events. Knowing what those events are will help you to put your course reading into context.
- Reading newspapers and magazines provides you with reading practice.
- Reading about current events helps you to understand how people assemble their arguments.

Apply the Strategy

Find a weekly news magazine and bring it to class. Read one of the main news articles in it. Complete the following information, and discuss the article with your class:

Title: _____

Magazine: _____

Brief Summary: _____
_____

What controversies are there over this topic? _____
_____

What groups of people are involved? _____

What connections do you see to any of your college courses? _____
_____

Test-Taking Tips offer students practical steps for improving their test results.

Check Your Progress helps students monitor their own progress.

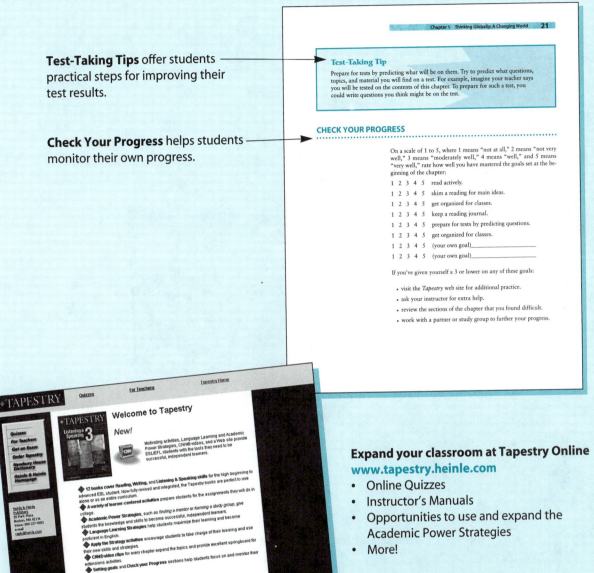

Test-Taking Tip

Prepare for tests by predicting what will be on them. Try to predict what questions, topics, and material you will find on a test. For example, imagine your teacher says you will be tested on the contents of this chapter. To prepare for such a test, you could write questions you think might be on the test.

CHECK YOUR PROGRESS

On a scale of 1 to 5, where 1 means "not at all," 2 means "not very well," 3 means "moderately well," 4 means "well," and 5 means "very well," rate how well you have mastered the goals set at the beginning of the chapter:

1 2 3 4 5   read actively.

1 2 3 4 5   skim a reading for main ideas.

1 2 3 4 5   get organized for classes.

1 2 3 4 5   keep a reading journal.

1 2 3 4 5   prepare for tests by predicting questions.

1 2 3 4 5   get organized for classes.

1 2 3 4 5   (your own goal)_____

1 2 3 4 5   (your own goal)_____

If you've given yourself a 3 or lower on any of these goals:

- visit the *Tapestry* web site for additional practice.
- ask your instructor for extra help.
- review the sections of the chapter that you found difficult.
- work with a partner or study group to further your progress.

Expand your classroom at Tapestry Online
www.tapestry.heinle.com
- Online Quizzes
- Instructor's Manuals
- Opportunities to use and expand the Academic Power Strategies
- More!

For a well-integrated curriculum, try the **Tapestry Writing** series and the **Tapestry Listening & Speaking** series, also from Heinle & Heinle.

To learn more about the **Tapestry** principles, read *The Tapestry of Language Learning,* Second Edition, by Rebecca L. Oxford and Robin C. Scarcella, also from Heinle & Heinle Publishers. ISBN 0-8384-0994-6.

Look at the photos. Then talk about these questions with your class:

- What are these people doing?
- Why do many adults go to school?
- Why do you go to school?
- What is your dream for the future?

COLLEGE LIFE: DIFFICULT DREAMS

College is a dream for many students. However, it is not an easy dream. In this chapter, you will read about college dreams and about education and jobs. You will also learn how to be a better student by learning about college classrooms.

Setting Goals

In this chapter, you will learn how to:

◈ use an English dictionary.

◈ preview your reading.

◈ make a study plan.

◈ make a reading notebook.

◈ keep a Vocabulary Log.

◈ preview test questions.

Which goal is most important to you? _____

_____

Why? _____

Talk about your answers with your class.

3

LANGUAGE LEARNING STRATEGY

Preview your reading to understand it better. To *preview* means to look at something before you study it. Previewing will help you think about your reading. It will help you understand the reading better, because you think about the ideas before you read.

Apply the Strategy

Preview this chapter. Talk with your class about these questions:

1. What is this chapter about?

2. How many readings are there?

3. What sections are in this chapter?

4. What is a strategy?

5. What are the two Language Learning Strategies?

6. What is the Academic Power Strategy?

7. What is the CNN video?

> **Learning is a treasure that will follow its owner everywhere.**
>
> **—CHINESE PROVERB**

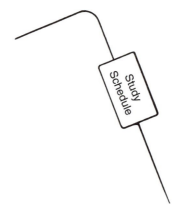

Study Schedule

Getting Started

Before you start this chapter, make a Reading Notebook for your notes and assignments. Make five sections, and use a divider for each section:

a. *Study plan*   You will learn more about how to make a study plan in this chapter. Keep a plan for each week in this section.

b. *Vocabulary Log*   Write all of the new words you learn in this part of your notebook. You will learn more about Vocabulary Logs in this chapter.

c. *Language Learning Strategies*   Each chapter in this book will have two Language Learning Strategies. Each Language Learning Strategy has two parts: first, the explanation of the strategy; second, an activity to help you learn the strategy better. Keep notes on the activities from the Language Learning Strategies here.

d. *Academic Power Strategies*   Each chapter in this book will have one Academic Power Strategy. Like the Language Learning Strategies, the Academic Power Strategies have two parts. Keep notes on the activities from the Academic Power Strategies here.

e. *Journal*   You will learn more about keeping a journal in Chapter 2. Keep all of your journal writing in this part.

◀ Getting Ready to Read

For many people, college is a dream. They know they will get a better job and be happier in their lives if they finish college. Ask three students these questions. Write their answers in the chart.

	Student 1	Student 2	Student 3
1. Why are you in school?			
2. Is college important to you? Why?			
3. What job do you want after college?			

Discuss the answers with your class.

Vocabulary Check

Look at the words and phrases below. Put a check mark next to the words that you know. Talk with your teacher and classmates about the words and phrases you don't know. Write the new words you learn in your Vocabulary Log.

_____ achieved	_____ envelope	_____ organization
_____ application	_____ fields	_____ picking
_____ backpack	_____ honor roll	_____ pilot
_____ congratulations	_____ hopeless	_____ praised
_____ encouraged	_____ mirror	_____ scars

LANGUAGE LEARNING STRATEGY

Use an English dictionary to learn more about English words. A dictionary gives you more than the meaning of a word. When you look up a word in the dictionary, you may also find information about pronunciation, the part of speech, and different forms of the word. You may also find a sentence to help you understand the word. For example, here is a dictionary entry for the word "semester."

> **se•mes•ter** /səˈmɛstər/ *n.* half of the school year: *I took intermediate German in the fall semester and advanced German in the spring semester.*

Apply the Strategy

You can use your dictionary to learn important information about English words. Use your dictionary to look up the words in the list in the Vocabulary Check activity. In the Vocabulary Log section of your notebook, write:

1. The new word. Copy it carefully to learn its spelling.

2. The part of speech of the word (noun, verb, adjective, adverb). Sometimes, a word might have more than one part of speech. For example, "scar" is both a verb and a noun. You can tell which part of speech a word might be by its place in a sentence or by the words that go with it. For example, if you see "the scar," you know "scar" is a noun, because only nouns go with the article "the."

3. The other forms of the word, and identify them. For example, "scar" has the forms "scarred" (adjective or past tense verb) and "scarring" (noun, verb, or adjective).

4. The definition of the word. Don't just copy the definition from the dictionary. Use your own words. This will help you understand the definition better.

5. The sentence in which the word is found in the reading. This will help you understand the word better, because you see how it is used.

6. A sentence of your own using the new word. When you practice using the word, you will remember it better.

Here is an example of a Vocabulary Log item:

WORD: scar (noun, verb)

OTHER FORMS: scarred, scarring

DEFINITION: a mark on the skin after a cut; to mark something

SENTENCE FROM THE READING: "In the mirror, he saw the scars on his hands, arms, and face."

OWN SENTENCE: After I cut my hand, I had a small scar.

 Read

Reading 1: The Dreams of Eduardo Ortega

1   It was a cold morning, and Eduardo Ortega was nervous. He held a large **envelope.** In it was his dream. But now, he was too nervous to open it.

2   "This is everything," he said. "I've worked for this since I was a young boy."

3   But Eduardo was no longer a boy. In the **mirror,** he saw the **scars** on his hands, arms, and face. He looked much older than he really was. He remembered the long hours working in the **fields, picking** strawberries and beans.

4   During those years, Eduardo became much more than a child worker. He became an excellent student. After the workday, his tired friends drank coffee or slept. Eduardo studied, read, and wrote

poetry and short stories. Although he missed many classes, he became the school's best student.

5   One school year, Eduardo **achieved** one of his dreams—to fly on an airplane for the first time. He wrote an essay that won a prize—a trip to San Francisco. As he flew, he felt free from his life of hard work in the fields. He promised himself not to return to that life. He loved to fly.

6   So this morning, he put the envelope into his **backpack** and caught the school bus.

7   When Eduardo started school, he knew only a few English words. But he studied hard in his English classes. Within two years, he was on the **honor roll.** Teachers **praised** him for his **organization** and intelligence. His high school English teacher knew he would become a college student.

8   Eduardo arrived at school with the envelope. He walked past his classmates and sat down in the cafeteria. He tore open the envelope and began reading the letter inside. It was the answer to his **application** to the state university. It was also the answer to beginning his dream of becoming a **pilot.**

9   Even though Eduardo worked to help his family, his father always **encouraged** him to go to school. So, while he worked, he also studied. Many days, he thought it was **hopeless.** He was too tired to read his books. But his father just smiled and told him he could do it.

10   Eduardo knew that his dream was his father's dream, too. His father was a smart man, but he was too poor to go to college. He loved to read, but never had time, because he worked long hours.

11   Eduardo's education was important for all of his family. He was the oldest. If he went to college, his brother and sister would go, too.

12   So, now, as he read the words, "**Congratulations** . . . you have been accepted," he knew that his dream was not lost. One day, he would be a pilot, flying every day to all the exciting places in the world.

◆**After You Read**

Discuss the following questions with your classmates:

1. Who is Eduardo Ortega?

2. Why is he nervous?

3. Why does Eduardo look older than he is?

4. What kind of work did Eduardo do when he was a child?

5. When did Eduardo study?

6. Why did Eduardo go to San Francisco?

7. What was in the envelope?

8. What is Eduardo's dream?

9. Do you think Eduardo's sister and brother will go to college? Why or why not?

10. How did Eduardo's father help his family?

TUNING IN: "ESL School"

© CNN

The CNN Video "ESL School" is about a program at William McKinley School in Burbank, California. Before you watch the video, look up the word "literacy" in your dictionary and discuss the phrase "family literacy" with your class. What do you think "family literacy" means?

As you watch "ESL School," check the items that you see in the video.

_____ adults reading books

_____ adults taking a test

_____ adults and children reading together

_____ ESL students talking

_____ adults and children writing

_____ ESL students listening to tapes

_____ teachers talking

_____ children eating lunch

Read the questions, then watch the video again to find the answers.

1. What are the adults reading?

    a. magazines   c. novels

    b. children's books   d. newspapers

2. How old is this program?

    a. 5 years   c. 20 years

    b. 15 years   d. 25 years

3. Which language skill is the most important, according to this video?

    a. speaking   c. reading

    b. listening   d. writing

Discuss these questions with your class:

1. Why do parents and children study together in the program?

2. Would you like to participate in this program? Why or why not?

◀ Getting Ready to Read

> A man who has never gone to school may steal from a freight car, but if he has a university education he may steal the whole railroad.
>
> **—FRANKLIN D. ROOSEVELT**

Before you read "Rules in the College Classroom," discuss these questions with your class:

1. What are the rules in your classroom?

2. Why are there classroom rules?

3. Are college rules different from high school rules? If so, why? Give an example.

4. With a partner, write five rules for a college classroom. Compare the rules you wrote with the rules written by your classmates. Which ones are helpful?

    1. _____

    2. _____

    3. _____

    4. _____

    5. _____

ACADEMIC POWER STRATEGY

Make a study plan to become a better student. Making a study plan will help you find time to study each week. On your study plan, write down the times that you go to classes, the times that you work, and other things that you do every week. Then look at your chart and decide on the days and times you can study. There is an example of a study schedule on the next page.

			DAY				
TIME	**Monday**	**Tuesday**	**Wednesday**	**Thursday**	**Friday**	**Saturday**	**Sunday**
7:00		*study*		*study*			
8:00	Math	↓	Math	↓	Math	job	
9:00	↓	English	↓	English	↓		baseball
10:00	*study*	↓	*study*	↓	*study*		↓
11:00	↓	↓	↓	↓	↓		
12:00	lunch	lunch	lunch	lunch	lunch		
1:00	Biology	Music	Biology	Music			
2:00	↓	↓	↓	↓	job		
3:00	↓	↓	↓	↓	↓		↓
4:00		piano practice		piano practice	↓	↓	
5:00							
6:00	*study*		*study*				*study*
7:00	↓	*study*	↓	*study*	*study*		↓
8:00		↓		↓	↓		
9:00	↓	↓	↓	↓	↓		↓
10:00							

(continued on the next page)

Apply the Strategy   Use the chart below to make your own study schedule.

TIME	DAY						
	Monday	Tuesday	Wednesday	Thursday	Friday	Saturday	Sunday
7:00							
8:00							
9:00							
10:00							
11:00							
12:00							
1:00							
2:00							
3:00							
4:00							
5:00							
6:00							
7:00							
8:00							
9:00							
10:00							

Vocabulary Check

Look at the words below. Put a check mark next to the words that you know. Talk with your class about the words you don't know. Write the new words you learn in your Vocabulary Log.

_____ attendance	_____ dropped	_____ punctual
_____ chew	_____ expect	_____ regularly
_____ considerate	_____ expectations	_____ requirements
_____ courteous	_____ policies	_____ responsibilities
_____ distracts	_____ prepared	_____ syllabus

One-third of college students are over 25 years old.

Read

Reading 2: Rules in the College Classroom

1   Most classrooms have rules. Even college classrooms have rules. Although they may be different from rules in high school classrooms, they are still important. Understanding the rules of the classroom will help you be a successful student.

2   What are your **responsibilities** as a student in a college classroom? First, you should be **prepared** for class. Read your assignments and finish your homework before coming to class. Next, you should be **punctual** and attend class **regularly.** Finally, you should be **courteous** and **considerate.** Don't talk, **chew** gum, or eat in class. Don't walk around or leave the class before asking the instructor.

3　Different teachers have different **policies** about the following things. Make sure you understand your teachers' policies.

Attendance and Punctuality

4　Most colleges have **attendance** rules. At some colleges, you may be **dropped** for not attending classes, so ask your teachers about these policies. Missing classes is serious. You might miss an assignment, a quiz, a review for a test, or special information about an assignment. If you miss a class, you must find out what you missed. Ask someone in the class to help you.

5　Punctuality means that you come to class on time. Being late **distracts** the other students and the instructor. If you come to class late, make as little noise as possible. Some instructors will not even allow you to enter class late. Another important aspect of punctuality is handing work in on time. Some instructors will not allow you to hand in work late. Know your instructors' rules.

Great Expectations

6　Know what your instructors **expect** of you. Different instructors will have different **requirements** and **expectations.** At the beginning of the semester, each of your instructors will tell you his or her expectations, requirements, and policies. Make sure you understand these. Ask questions if you don't understand. At the beginning of the semester, your instructor will give you a written **syllabus.** This syllabus includes attendance and grading policies and assignment schedules. Read the syllabus and make sure you understand it.

Be Prepared

7　Be prepared for each class. Finish your homework before class and be ready to hand in any work due. Do not do your homework during class. Eat, use the restroom, make phone calls, and unpack your books, notebooks, and pencils before class starts.

Class Notebooks

8　It is important to have a notebook for each class or one notebook with dividers for each class. Taking notes is important in college. You should have an organized place to put all of your notes and class handouts.

—Adapted from Lynda Corbin, City Times, Dec.1993

After You Read

Read through "Rules in the College Classroom" again.

1. Write down as many rules for the college classroom as you can find in the reading.

   _____

   _____

   _____

   _____

   _____

   _____

2. Select three of the rules that you think are most important. Share your ideas with your class.

   1. _____

   2. _____

   3. _____

3. Why are these rules important or helpful for students?

4. Compare the rules you picked with the rules you wrote before the reading. Are they the same?

Vocabulary Building

Match the word with its meaning. Draw a line to the correct meaning. One is done for you.

1. attendance	hope
2. chew	being present
3. considerate	rules
4. distract	look forward to
5. expect	take one's attention from
6. expectation	ready
7. policies	thoughtful
8. prepared	class plan
9. punctual	bite
10. regularly	duties
11. responsibilities	constantly
12. syllabus	on time

◆ **Grammar You Can Use**

Imperative Verbs

Use imperative verbs to give instructions or to tell someone to do something.

The imperative form is the base form or dictionary form of the verb. In the reading "Rules in the College Classroom," there are many instructions or rules which use the imperative form. Here is one sentence:

> "**Read** your assignments and **complete** your homework before coming to class."

The two imperative verbs in this sentence are "read" and "complete." These verbs tell the students what to do before they come to class.

A two-year community college degree can increase your income by one-third. A four-year degree can increase it by two-thirds.

1. Look at the reading again. Underline all of the imperative verbs that you can find.

2. Look at the rules that you wrote in the Getting Ready to Read activity. Did you use imperative verbs? Rewrite any rules that don't have imperative verbs.

Test-Taking Tip

Preview all the questions on a test before you begin the test. Previewing will help you:

- answer easier questions first.

- plan your time.

- think about difficult questions.

- feel more confident.

◆ **Getting Ready to Read**

What jobs require a college education? With a partner, make a list of ten jobs that require a college education. One example is given for you.

doctor	

Compare your list with those your classmates made. How many different jobs did you and your classmates list?

Vocabulary Check

Look at the words and phrases below. Put a check mark next to the words or phrases that you know. Talk with your class about the words and phrases you don't know. Write the new words you learn in your Vocabulary Log.

_____ administrators	_____ factory	_____ reports
_____ advice	_____ fast food	_____ shocked
_____ amazing	_____ global economy	_____ technology
_____ average	_____ incomes	_____ wages
_____ connection	_____ janitor	_____ waiters
_____ cure	_____ living standards	_____ waste
_____ enemy	_____ printer	

◆Read

This reading is the text from a radio report. Different people, including reporters, are talking about jobs and education.

Reading 3: Education and Income

1 JOHN MCMANN, Host: This is the morning news; I'm John McMann. Since World War II, Americans have believed that **living standards** would improve. Most parents hoped that their children would live better lives than they did. For millions of Americans, that dream has not come true. During the past 20 years, poor people's **incomes** have fallen. Those in the middle have worked harder but seen no increases. Marie Shelton **reports** this story.

2   MARIE SHELTON: Here's an **amazing** fact: Today, a 30-year-old man with a high school education makes about $7,000 less than a similar man 15 years ago. His **wages** fell from $28,000 a year in 1979 to about $21,000 a year in 1996, after adjustment for inflation.[1] Sixty-five percent of workers have a high school education or less.

[1]Inflation is the increase of prices. You can't compare prices in 1970 with prices in 2000 because of inflation. So, in order to compare prices, you must adjust for inflation.

3   TIMOTHY CALDWELL: My name is Timothy Caldwell, and I'm 36 years old. I'm single.

4   MARIE SHELTON: At a **fast food** restaurant in Boston, Timothy Caldwell, a single father with a high school education, thinks about the past six years of his life. He says it's been hard to find a good-paying job.

5   TIMOTHY CALDWELL: It seems like every time I found a good job and felt happy, they quickly went out of business.[2] After I lost my last job, I had to take minimum-wage[3] jobs. They are terrible jobs.

6   MARIE SHELTON: In the late 1980s, Caldwell had a good job. He worked as a **printer,** making $30,000 a year. He quit with the dream of starting his own printing business. When that didn't succeed, he looked for a new job. He found work as a **janitor,** working 20 hours a week for $4.25 an hour. He knows he needs a better education.

7   TIMOTHY CALDWELL: I asked myself, 'Can I go to college? What would it be like to study instead of work?' But I hadn't saved enough money. I have a daughter, so I have to work.

[2]To "go out of business" means to close down a company. Usually, a company goes out of business because there aren't enough customers or there are other problems.

[3]Minimum wage is the lowest hourly pay that a worker can be paid legally in the United States. The government decides on the minimum wage.

8   MARIE SHELTON: Twenty years ago, young men like Caldwell could have finished high school and gotten a well-paying job in a **factory.** Of course, many of those jobs are gone today, and there are more service jobs, like those in restaurants and stores. And today, education is more important than ever. The U.S. Labor Secretary[4] says that just 15 years ago, the **average** male college graduate earned 50 percent more than a worker with a high school education. Today, college graduates earn 96 percent more. He says there are two reasons for this change.

9   LABOR SECRETARY: If you have the right skills, **technology** and the **global economy** are on your side. You can help the global economy. On the other hand, if you don't have the right skills or the right education, technology may be your **enemy.**

10   MARIE SHELTON: The answer, economists agree, is to improve the education level of the nation's workers. But many of today's workers aren't prepared. When they were in school, jobs were different. In the 1970s, a college education didn't pay well because there were too many educated workers. College-educated workers were a dime a dozen.[5] Many high school students were told, "College doesn't pay." That quickly changed, of course, as the economy changed. But it took a long time for students to understand this. In the 1980s, college graduates were getting good wages and some high school students were getting bad **advice.** Karen Miller, an economist from the University of Texas, studies the **connection** between education and income.

11   KAREN MILLER: In the late 1980s, I talked to a group of school **administrators** from around the country. I told them that a college education was important for a good job. They were **shocked.** They were telling students that college graduates became taxi drivers or **waiters.** They told students not to go to college! They said it was a **waste** of money. A lot of people didn't understand the truth.

12   MARIE SHELTON: So, it's an open-and-shut case. Better education is the **cure** for America's wage problems. But even though

[4]The U.S. Labor Secretary is the person in charge of the U.S. government's Department of Labor.

[5]"A dime a dozen" means that there is a large supply of something and it's very cheap.

most economists believe that, it's not always that simple. We'll report on part two of this story tomorrow.

13   JOHN MCMANN: Thank you, Marie.

After You Read

1. What dream do many American parents have for their children?

2. In the first paragraph, who are "those in the middle"?

3. How have incomes changed in the last twenty years?

4. Why didn't Timothy Caldwell go to college?

5. What is an example of a minimum-wage job?

6. If Timothy Caldwell had worked twenty years ago, where could he have found a job?

7. What did the Labor Secretary say about jobs and education?

8. When were there too many educated workers?

9. Why did many high school students not go to college in the 1980s?

10. What did Karen Miller learn when she talked to school administrators?

11. What will solve the wage problems in the U.S.?

Vocabulary Building

This reading contains some *idioms*. Idioms often are not found in a dictionary. Also, although you may know all the words in an idiom, its meaning might not be clear. Discuss these idioms with a partner. Put the idiom into your own words.

1. an open-and-shut case _____

   _____

2. went out of business _____

   _____

3. on my side _____

   _____

4. on the other hand _____

   _____

5. a dime a dozen _____

   _____

Next, choose the correct idiom from the list to put into the sentences below.

1. I really want to go to college; _____ I have to work.

2. The economy is _____; I should be able to find a good job after college.

3. The restaurant _____, so I lost my job.

4. Waiters are _____, so I'm sure they'll find another one.

5. It's _____! College pays!

PUTTING IT ALL TOGETHER

> There are few earthly things more beautiful than a university . . . a place where those who hate ignorance may strive to know, where those who perceive truth may strive to make others see.
>
> **—JOHN MASEFIELD**

Read the paragraph below, written by Roya, a new student at a local community college. She has a very busy schedule, and worries that she may not be a successful student.

My name is Roya. I would like to study child development so that I can start my own business: a day care center. I want to finish my studies quickly because I want to have a better job and earn more money. Since I want to finish in two years, I have to take 4 classes each semester. However, I must also work to pay for my classes and for my living expenses. I get financial aid, but it is not enough to pay for everything. I work 20 hours a week to pay for my rent, car, food, and tuition. Also, my family is very important to me. I have to visit them on the weekends; otherwise, they will worry about me. Finally, I need time to enjoy myself. I like to exercise and I like to go to the movies with my friends. Is it possible to be a successful student with such a busy schedule? How can I reach my goal and still enjoy my life?

Can Roya become a successful student? Do the following:

1. Look at Roya's schedule on the next page. When are some good times for her to study? Mark some study times on her schedule. (Remember, Roya has four classes to study for.)

2. Now mark her free time.

3. Do you think she can be a successful student? Do you have any suggestions for Roya about how to become a successful student? What are they?

	DAY						
TIME	**Monday**	**Tuesday**	**Wednesday**	**Thursday**	**Friday**	**Saturday**	**Sunday**
7:00	exercise	exercise	exercise	exercise	exercise	exercise	
8:00	class		class		class		
9:00	class		class		class		
10:00	class	class	class	class	class	work	visit parents
11:00	class	class	class	class	class	work	
12:00							
1:00	work	class	work	class	work		
2:00	work	class	work	class	work		
3:00	work		work		work		
4:00	work		work		work		↓
5:00	work		work		work		
6:00	work		work		work		
7:00							
8:00							
9:00							
10:00							

CHECK YOUR PROGRESS

On a scale of 1 to 5, where 1 means "not at all," 2 means "not very well," 3 means "moderately well," 4 means "well," and 5 means "very well," rate how well you have mastered the goals set at the beginning of the chapter:

1 2 3 4 5   use an English dictionary.

1 2 3 4 5   preview your reading.

1 2 3 4 5   make a study plan.

1 2 3 4 5   make a reading notebook.

1 2 3 4 5   keep a Vocabulary Log.

1 2 3 4 5   preview test questions.

If you've given yourself a 3 or lower on any of these goals:

- visit the *Tapestry* web site for additional practice.
- ask your instructor for extra help.
- review the sections of the chapter that you found difficult.
- work with a partner or study group to further your progress.

L ook at the photo. Then discuss these questions with your classmates:

- Where does this photo take place?
- What is the woman in the photo doing?
- Do you bring water with you to class?

WATER: OUR MOST IMPORTANT RESOURCE

Water is important to all life on earth. Water keeps us healthy, keeps plants and animals alive, and keeps things clean. However, water itself sometimes is not clean. Keeping our water safe and clean is important to many people. This chapter gives some information about the water we drink, and how we can protect it.

Setting Goals

In this chapter, you will learn how to:

◆ scan for information.

◆ understand implied ideas.

◆ keep a reading journal.

◆ use "how much" and "how many."

◆ answer easy questions first on a test.

Which goal is most important to you?_____

_____

Why?_____

Talk about your answers with your class.

**Getting Started**

Before you begin this chapter, read the questions in the chart. With your class, discuss any words that you do not understand. Then ask three classmates these questions. Write their answers in the chart.

	Student 1	Student 2	Student 3
How much water do you drink every day?			
Do you drink bottled water?			
Why or why not?			

After you complete the chart, talk about the answers with your class. Answer these questions:

1. How much water do all of your classmates drink every day?

2. Do most of your classmates drink bottled water?

3. Why or why not?

Getting Ready to Read

The first reading, "Water Facts," is a chart. It gives information about how much water different things need. Before you read the chart, think about these questions:

- What things in your house need or use water (for example, plants, animals, washing machines, dishwashers, and so on)? Think of five things and put them in the following chart.

- How much water do you think they need or use? Fill in the right column with your answers.

Measurement Chart

U.S. MEASUREMENTS		METRIC MEASUREMENTS
1 TEASPOON	=	5 MILLILITERS
1 TABLESPOON	=	15 MILLILITERS
1 CUP	=	250 MILLILITERS
1 PINT	=	500 MILLILITERS
1 QUART	=	1 LITER
1 GALLON	=	3.8 LITERS

Thing	Amount of Water Used
1.	
2.	
3.	
4.	
5.	

Compare your answers with your classmates. Answer these questions:

1. Did you give the same answers?

2. Which answers were different?

3. Why are they different?

4. Do you want to change any of your answers?

LANGUAGE LEARNING STRATEGY

Scan to find information quickly. When you scan, you do not read every word. Instead, you look quickly at a reading in order to find certain facts or ideas. Think of a question before you scan. For example, you may want to know how long a camel can go without water. In that case, you would read quickly and notice only the sections related to this information. You would ignore other parts of the reading that do not answer your question.

Apply the Strategy

Scan "Water Facts" and answer these questions:

1. Which thing uses 2–7 gallons of water?

2. How much water does a football field use in a day?

3. How does a tree use water?

4. How much water does a giant saguaro cactus use in a day?

5. How much water does an oak tree use in a day?

6. Which animal or thing uses the most water?

7. Which animal or thing uses the least water?

Vocabulary Check

Look at the words below. Put a check mark next to the words that you know. Talk with your class about the words and phrases you don't know. Write the new words you learn in your Vocabulary Log.

_____ absorbs	_____ dew	_____ pump
_____ cactus	_____ flush	_____ roots
_____ cycle	_____ gills	

Read   **Reading 1: Water Facts**

Thing	Average Amount of Water Needed	Thing	Average Amount of Water Needed
dishwasher	9–12 gallons for one wash cycle	freshwater fish	None—fish don't drink water. It enters their bodies through their skin and gills, but they pump it out again.
washing machine	50 gallons for one wash cycle	garbage disposal	1 gallon for one minute
toilet	2–7 gallons for one flush	giant saguaro cactus	1 gallon every day—the cactus absorbs dew through its roots.
shower	25–50 gallons for a five-minute shower	football field	7,140 gallons every day
person	2.5 quarts a day (from both drinking and eating)	oak tree	88 gallons every day—the tree absorbs most of its water through its roots.

After You Read

Talk about these questions with your class.

1. What facts in the chart were most interesting to you?

2. What facts in the chart surprised you?

3. How do humans get the water they need?

4. Do you use more or less water than the average person?

5. What are the ways you use water each day?

Grammar You Can Use

"How Much" and "How Many"

When you want to ask a question about the amount of something, use "how much" or "how many."

Use "how many" with count nouns. Count nouns are nouns that have a plural form. For example, "cup" is a count noun, so you can use "how many" with this noun in its plural form. You can ask, "How many cups of water does a human drink each day?"

Use "how much" with non-count nouns. Non-count nouns are nouns that do not have a plural form. For example, "water" is a non-count noun, so you should use "how much" with it. You can ask, "How much water do you drink each day?" Here are some nouns from the "Water Facts" chart. Are they count or non-count nouns? Write a "C" by the count nouns, and an "N" by the non-count nouns.

> There is the same amount of water on Earth today as there was when the Earth was formed. The water from your faucet could contain molecules that dinosaurs drank.

_____ quart   _____ field   _____ gallon   _____ dew

_____ water   _____ cactus   _____ skin   _____ tree

Now write questions with these nouns using either "how much" or "how many." One is done for you.

1. <u>How many quarts of water does a dog drink every day?</u>

2. _____

3. _____

4. _____

5. _____

6. _____

7. _____

8. _____

◆ Vocabulary Building

Write the correct word in the blanks. Cross them off when you use them.

absorbs   cactus   roots

gills   cycle

1. A _____ does not use much water.

2. A towel _____ a lot of water.

3. Water enters fish through their _____.

4. One _____ in a dishwasher is enough to get dishes clean.

5. Trees get water through their _____.

◆ Getting Ready to Read

The next reading discusses the safety of your drinking water. Before you read, talk about these questions with your class:

1. Do you know where your water at school comes from?

2. How could you find out where it comes from?

3. Have you ever had your water tested?

4. Do you think bottled water is safer than tap water?

A person can live about a month without food, but only about a week without water.

Vocabulary Check

Look at the words and phrases below. Put a check mark next to the words and phrases that you know. Talk with your class about the ones that you don't know. Write the new words you learn in your Vocabulary Log.

_____ bacteria	_____ laboratory	_____ statistics
_____ categories	_____ lead (noun)	_____ tap water
_____ chemicals	_____ officials	_____ threats
_____ damage	_____ plumbing	_____ treatment
_____ filtered	_____ protection	_____ wells
_____ garbage dump	_____ raw sewage	
_____ label	_____ samples	

ACADEMIC POWER STRATEGY

Keep a reading journal to think about your ideas and your learning. Sometimes your teacher may ask you to write about what you read. Keeping your writing in a journal will help you to review your ideas, remember your reading, and understand what you have read.

Apply the Strategy

In Chapter 1, you made a section in your reading notebook for your journal. When you read the next article, "How Safe is Your Water?" write down questions or ideas you have. For example, what things do you agree with or disagree with? Then, after you have finished, write a paragraph about the reading. Write about your own ideas and questions about the reading. You may add questions about anything you didn't understand. Your teacher may ask you to share your paragraph with the class. Keep your writing in the journal section of your reading notebook.

 Read

Reading 2: How Safe Is Your Water?

1 Molly Arnold, a young mother in Virginia, decided to have her **tap water** tested. Her report came back from the **laboratory** with bad news. "Since then we haven't drunk our tap water," she says. "We haven't for three years."

2 The lab said that there was too much **lead** in her water—more than twice as much as there should be. Ms. Arnold doesn't have enough money for new pipes in her home. She knows that if she drinks water with lead in it, she might **damage** her health. She has a two-year-old son and she worries about him, too. So, she brings drinking water by car from her mother's house.

3 Many people worry about their drinking water. While government **officials** say the water is safe, many people don't believe them. Last year, Americans spent over two billion dollars on bottled water and 450 million dollars on home **treatment** systems.

4 "There is a large part of the population in the 20th century who don't drink from their own taps," says Barbara Chung, a water expert for the Water **Protection** Group. "We have not improved our drinking water treatment system."

5   For about half of all Americans, tap water comes from lakes and rivers. For another 35 percent, it comes from underground waterways called *aquifers*. The remaining 15 percent of Americans use private **wells,** which are not controlled. But it doesn't matter where we get our water, because any source can become polluted.

6   Even if you buy your water at the store, you can't be sure that it is safe. The biggest **threats** to the nation's water supply include three **categories** of pollution. Normal treatment does not remove any of these:

    Chemicals from farming and factories: Chemicals have appeared in well water and lakes. They cause a lot of health problems.

    Lead: Lead is used in **plumbing.** Even small amounts can cause brain damage. Although lead pipes are no longer sold in the United States, lead is still allowed in new taps.

    *Germs and **bacteria**.* Water treatment plants give off 1.2 trillion[1] gallons of **raw sewage** every year. Much of this sewage goes into someone else's water supply. Raw sewage has a lot of germs and bacteria that can cause many diseases. The Environmental Protection Agency (EPA) says that about 17 percent of Americans live in towns that have water problems. Twelve million people use water that has not been **filtered.**

[1]One trillion = 1,000,000,000,000

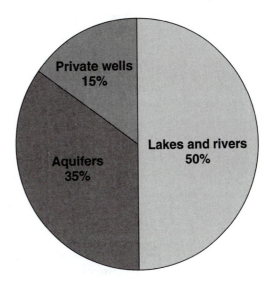

7   You might believe that someone is checking your water 24 hours a day. However, there are no requirements for daily, or even weekly, tests for chemicals, lead, or pesticides.[2] Each state has its own testing system, because the U.S. government doesn't have one. "It's not a national issue," says Carl Reeverts, from the EPA water programs. "It's a local issue."

8   So how do you know what's in your water? By law, you can ask local water officials. But they may not be able to talk about the problem in plain English. Many people don't understand water **statistics.** Sometimes, you don't get complete answers.

9   Henry Scarpetta had his water tested because he lives near a **garbage dump.** "You know how the government is," the 77-year-old doctor says. "You don't get all the answers right away." So Scarpetta sent water **samples** away for testing. The tests showed that his water is clean, but Scarpetta wants to be safe. He buys bottled water.

10   But is bottled water better? There were large amounts sold last year—2.43 billion gallons, or nine gallons for each American. Those Americans might be surprised to learn that 25% of all bottled water comes from the same rivers and lakes as tap water.

11   However, the best water companies try to make bottled water cleaner. If your tap water is polluted, bottled water is a good idea. Sometimes, however, government tests have found pollution in bottled water. So, even with bottled water, you must be careful.

[2]Pesticides are chemicals that kill insects.

12   If your bottled water says "*artesian*" on the **label**, it means the water comes from underground water, which may be less polluted. If your bottle says "*purified,*" your water has been specially treated. Both purified and artesian water have no lead in them.

13   Your drinking water may never be 100% safe. Testing your water will help you know if it's safe. And, if you drink bottled water, knowing how it is cleaned, and where it comes from, will help you stay healthy.

After You Read

1. Why doesn't Molly Arnold drink her tap water?

2. Why shouldn't you drink water with lead in it?

3. How much money did Americans spend on bottled water and treatment systems?

4. Where do most Americans get their drinking water?

5. What are the three categories of water pollution?

6. How many Americans drink water that is not filtered?

7. Does the U.S. government check water quality? Why or why not?

8. Why is it difficult to talk to local water officials?

9. Why does Mr. Scarpetta buy bottled water?

10. How much bottled water do Americans drink?

11. Why is *artesian* water usually safe?

12. What does *purified* water mean?

13. What should you do if you are worried about your water?

> **Growing a day's food for 1 adult takes about 1,700 gallons of water.**
>
> —NATIONAL GEOGRAPHIC SOCIETY

Vocabulary Building

Can you put these words into *categories*? Some words might fit into more than one category. Work with a partner. One is done for you.

bacteria	samples
chemicals	raw sewage
filter	statistics
garbage dump	tap
lead	the public
officials	wells
pipes	

Things you might find in a laboratory	Things related to plumbing	Words that refer to people	Things that are dirty
bacteria			

TUNING IN: "Water and Cancer"

Before you watch the CNN video "Water and Cancer," study the list of words and phrases below. Put a check mark next to the ones you know. Talk with your teacher and classmates about any words and phrases you don't know.

_____ at risk

_____ by-product

_____ cancer causing agents

_____ carcinogens

_____ charcoal filter

_____ chlorine

_____ research

While you are watching the video, write a list of the different places to get drinking water that you see in the video. After you watch, compare your list with the lists your classmates wrote. How many places to get drinking water are shown in the video?

Read the following questions and watch "Water and Cancer" again. Then answer these questions:

1. In the United States, what percentage of water gets chlorine treatment?

2. What kind of cancer could chlorinated water cause?

© CNN

3. Should we stop drinking tap water?

4. How can we make our drinking water safer at home?

Test-Taking Tip

Do easy questions first. Most tests have questions that are easy, medium, and difficult. However, the questions don't always come in that order. You should look for the easiest questions and do those first. This will help you save time to work on the more difficult questions later. It will also give you confidence to do the harder questions. Sometimes, easier questions help you remember ideas for the harder questions.

◆ Getting Ready to Read

In the next reading, "Waste Not, Want Not," the author uses *headings* to organize the information. Headings are like titles inside an essay. They tell you what the ideas in each part of the essay will be.

Scan the article "Waste Not, Want Not." Fill in the information in the chart:

Title:	
Heading 1:	
Heading 2:	
Heading 3:	

Can you guess what this reading is about from the headings?

Vocabulary Check

Look at the following words and phrases. Put a check mark next to the words and phrases that you know. Talk with your class about the ones you don't know. Write the new words you learn in your Vocabulary Log.

———— baseball fields ———— demand (noun) ———— golf courses

———— cheaper ———— effects (noun) ———— lawns

_____ led   _____ settlers   _____ struck

_____ precious   _____ ski resort   _____ unpleasant

_____ reclaimed   _____ slopes (noun)

 Read

Reading 3: Waste Not, Want Not

What is Water Reclamation?

1   In the 1980s, a drought **struck** California. California's water disappeared. This made officials look for other water sources. Their search **led** them to *wastewater reclamation*—using purified water from sewers instead of treated water for certain purposes. This became an important way of saving the **precious** water supply.

2   Although some people think using wastewater is **unpleasant,** it is a good way to increase local water supplies. In some areas, **reclaimed** wastewater (ReW) may be the only water for farming or watering **lawns.**

The History of Water Reclamation

3   Water has been reclaimed since the days of the first **settlers.** However, government water programs started in the 1960s in Colorado Springs, Colorado. They began watering city **golf courses** and other public areas with ReW.

4   During the 1970s, ReW projects grew. At first, people were worried wastewater would carry diseases. But, when wastewater

systems improved, more cities used ReW to increase local water supplies.

5   The California drought showed how important ReW is. ReW was used a lot during this time, with no negative health **effects.** People finally believed that ReW was safe. Today, every big city in Southern California has laws requiring ReW systems.

The Uses of ReW

6 Of course, people don't drink ReW, but it can be used for many other things. At the Snow Valley **ski resort,** officials want to use ReW to water the grass ski **slopes** in the summer and to make snow in the winter. However, high-quality water is needed for snow. For now, they still make snow with regular water. Many states—including California, Arizona, and Florida—require ReW to water public green areas. Golf courses need a lot of water to stay green. They use ReW because it is often **cheaper** than treated water.

7   "Golf courses, parks and **baseball fields** are important to the public," says Frank Jersey, of the National Golf Association. "By using reclaimed wastewater, golf courses can help save water. At the same time, the golf course or park is saving money in water costs."

8   When ReW is cheap, many people want to use it. A study in Florida showed that households would use up to 400 gallons for every person each day, if it were free. They will use it to water their lawns. This high **demand** exists even when ReW costs 85 percent of the drinking water prices.

9   So, although the idea of ReW may sound unpleasant to some people, it is safe and popular. It also keeps farms, parks, and golf courses green. It is a useful source of water, which will become even more important in the future.

◀ **After You Read**

1. Why did California officials have to find a new water source?

2. What is water reclamation?

3. Why do you think some people find reclaimed water unpleasant?

4. When and where did government water programs start?

5. Why were some people afraid of using wastewater?

6. What is ReW used for?

7. Why do golf courses use so much ReW?

8. How will people in Florida use ReW?

9. Why is ReW important?

10. Should your city have a ReW program? Why or why not?

◆ Vocabulary Building

> **80% of all public water is used for irrigation of crops.**
>
> —U.S. DEPT. OF ENERGY

baseball field	lawns
cheaper	precious
demand (noun)	reclaim
effects (noun)	ski resort
golf course	slopes (noun)
led	unpleasant

Write a paragraph about reclaimed water. Use at least six of the words from the list in your paragraph.

LANGUAGE LEARNING STRATEGY

Understand implied ideas in your reading. Readings sometimes contain ideas that aren't directly explained. These are hidden, or *implied,* ideas. Often the writer believes the readers will understand these ideas without an explanation. Recognizing and thinking about these implied ideas will help you understand your reading better.

Apply the Strategy

In "Waste Not, Want Not," the writer does not explain *why* some people find the idea of reclaimed water unpleasant. Talk about these questions with a partner:

1. What might be unpleasant about using reclaimed water?

2. Why didn't the writer explain this, in your opinion?

3. Imagine a friend finds using ReW unpleasant. Tell him why it is safe and useful.

PUTTING IT ALL TOGETHER

1. Look at columns A and B below. In each column, there are words in bold. Write a list of these words and discuss their meanings with your class.

2. Read columns A and B. Then match the question with the correct answer.

A	B
1. What are **wetlands**?	a. Wetlands are found all over the world, in every state of the U.S., in cities, in the country, by the oceans, and **inland.**
2. What are the main **ingredients** of wetlands?	b. They use wetlands for bird-watching, fishing, **canoeing, hunting,** and **photography.**
3. Where are wetlands found?	c. They are made up of water, soil that is always or sometimes soaked with water, and water-loving plants.
4. How do people enjoy wetlands?	d. Wetlands are areas that are both earth and water.

3. Do an Internet search using the keyword "wetlands" to learn more about wetlands.

CHECK YOUR PROGRESS

On a scale of 1 to 5, rate how well you've mastered the goals set at the beginning of the chapter:

1 2 3 4 5   scan for information.

1 2 3 4 5   understand implied ideas.

1 2 3 4 5   keep a reading journal.

1 2 3 4 5   use "how much" and "how many."

1 2 3 4 5   answer easy questions first on a test.

If you've given yourself a 3 or lower on any of these goals:

- visit the *Tapestry* web site for additional practice.
- ask your instructor for extra help.
- review the sections of the chapter that you found difficult.
- work with a partner or study group to further your progress.

L ook at the photos. Then discuss these questions with your
class:

- What do you do to stay healthy?
- Do you enjoy healthy food? Why or why not?
- Do you enjoy exercise? Why or why not?

3

HEALTHY HABITS

What is asthma? Is coffee bad for your health? Does chicken soup help cure the flu? This chapter will give you answers to these questions. It will also give you more information about healthy living.

Setting Goals

In this chapter, you will learn how to:

◆ find examples in your reading.

◆ skim to get the main idea.

◆ set realistic academic goals.

◆ do well on true-false tests.

◆ use correct grammar when you give advice.

Which goal is most important to you?_____

_____

Why?_____

Talk about your answers with your class.

◆**Getting Started**

Preview Chapter Three. Look quickly through it and answer these questions:

1. Which reading looks most interesting to you? _____

    _____

    Why? _____

    _____

2. Do you already know something about these topics? Check the ones you know about.

    _____ a. asthma   _____ c. home remedies

    _____ b. caffeine   _____ d. heart disease

Explain to a partner what you know about one of the topics you checked.

◆**Getting Ready to Read**

The first reading is about an Olympic athlete with asthma. Before you read it, think about what you already know about these subjects. With a group, answer the following questions. Write down the group's answers.

1. What are the Olympics?

2. Can you name some Olympic athletes?

3. What is the top prize in the Olympics?

4. What is asthma?

5. Do you know anyone with asthma?

6. Do you think many Olympic athletes have health problems? Why or why not?

Vocabulary Check

Look at the following list of words and phrases. Put a check mark next to the ones that you know. Talk with your class about the words and phrases you don't know. Write the new words you learn in your Vocabulary Log.

_____ admit   _____ festival   _____ panic

_____ asthma attack   _____ gold medal   _____ participate

_____ condition   _____ lungs   _____ proof

_____ severe   _____ stadium   _____ wheezing

_____ side effects _____ tough

Read

> Almost 12 million
> Americans have asthma.

Reading 1: Running with Asthma

1 Jackie Joyner-Kersee, an Olympic athlete, had a **severe asthma attack** while running a race at the 1994 U.S. Olympic **Festival.**

Jackie Joyner-Kersee

2 "I wasn't afraid of running; I was afraid I might die," said Joyner- Kersee. "I said, 'Don't **panic** . . . just hold on.' "

3 So, what is asthma? It's a health **condition** that makes it hard to breathe. Although it comes and goes, once you have asthma, you have it for a long time. Different treatments are used for asthma. There are very strong drugs that can be taken for a long time with few **side effects.** Today, even people with severe asthma can **participate** in sports.

4 Joyner-Kersee has had problems with asthma for many years. She said, "I didn't have this as a little girl. It wasn't until I went to California that I noticed it, and then I didn't want to accept it. When I start feeling good, I stop taking the medicine. It will be all right. . . . I hope."

5 The race was supposed to start at 5:35 p.m. At 5:00, she began to have trouble breathing. She was given a breathing test and treatment by a doctor. She said she thought about not running. She was **wheezing.**

6 "It's just **tough** running with asthma," she said. "When I experienced this in practice, it was scary…. I couldn't breathe. It was really tough for me." She said the problem with asthma is that you don't know when an attack will happen. She was fine when she arrived at the **stadium.** The breathing treatment helped her.

7 Joyner-Kersee is **proof** that medical treatment is important. First, if you think you have asthma, see a doctor. Asthma drugs can protect your **lungs.** Second, pay attention to your health. Tell your doctor immediately if you wake up and have trouble breathing. This means the condition is getting worse. Many people don't want to **admit** they have asthma, and then they must go to the hospital.

8 Most importantly, remember that with asthma, you can have a normal life. You can even win an Olympic **gold medal.**

After You Read

> The medals don't mean anything and the glory doesn't last. It's all about your happiness. The rewards are going to come, but my happiness is just loving the sport and having fun performing.
>
> —JACKIE JOYNER-KERSEE

1. Who is Jackie Joyner-Kersee?

2. What is her sport in the Olympics?

3. What is asthma?

4. How long has Joyner-Kersee had asthma?

5. How does her asthma affect her participation in sports?

6. How is her asthma treated?

7. What should you do if you think you have asthma?

8. How do asthma drugs help?

9. How can you tell if your asthma is getting worse?

10. Why do you think many people don't want to admit they have asthma?

Vocabulary Building

Put these words and phrases into the category "Olympic Athlete" or "Asthma." Some words might belong in both categories. One is done for you.

attack	gold medal	participate	stadium
condition	lungs	severe	tough
festival	panic	side effects	wheezing

Olympic Athlete	Asthma
	attack

LANGUAGE LEARNING STRATEGY

Find examples to understand important ideas in your reading. Writers need to show that what they say is true. They often use examples to help them explain a fact. Here are some facts and examples from the last reading. They give the reader more information about asthma:

> *Fact:* Once you have asthma, you have it for a long time.
> *Example:* Joyner-Kersee has had problems with asthma for many years.
> *Fact:* Medical treatment is important.
> *Example:* The breathing treatment helped Joyner-Kersee.

Apply The Strategy

Look for other facts and examples in the reading. Work with a partner.

Underline each fact.

Double underline each example that goes with the fact.

Talk about your answers with your class.

◆ Getting Ready to Read

The next reading is about "home remedies." Home remedies are simple treatments for illnesses which you can do for yourself. Preview the reading "Home Remedies." Five health problems are listed in bold and underlined. Write the five health problems here:

1. _____
2. _____
3. _____
4. _____
5. _____

What do you do when you have one of these health problems? Discuss your answers to this question with your class.

Vocabulary Check

Look at the list of words and phrases on the next page. Put a check mark next to the ones you know. Talk with your class about the

Regular exercise can help protect you from heart disease and stroke, high blood pressure, diabetes, obesity, back pain, osteoporosis, and can improve your mood and help you manage stress better. For the greatest overall health benefits, experts recommend that you do 20 to 30 minutes of aerobic activity three or more times a week and some type of muscle strengthening activity at least twice a week.

words and phrases you don't know. Write the new words you learn in your Vocabulary Log.

_____ baking soda	_____ lukewarm	_____ remedy
_____ bee stings	_____ motion sickness	_____ soaking
_____ effective	_____ nausea	_____ stings
_____ ginger	_____ oatmeal	_____ sunburn
_____ insomnia	_____ paste	_____ symptoms
_____ itchy	_____ pressure	_____ thumbnail

◆**Read**

Reading 2: Home Remedies

1   What is a home **remedy?** It's a simple way to treat an illness at home, without medicine. Throughout history, there have been many home remedies. Some don't work, or are dangerous. For example, one home remedy advises you to put butter on a burn. This will make the burn worse, however, not better.

2   So how do you know which home remedies really work? Scientists believe that these home remedies really are **effective**:

Chicken Soup for <u>Colds</u>.

3   For a long time, doctors have recommended drinking any hot liquid to relieve cold **symptoms.** However, research shows that hot chicken soup is especially helpful.

A Hot Bath for <u>Insomnia</u>.

4   When you can't sleep, a nice hot bath before bedtime can help. In one study, nine women with **insomnia** took a hot bath $1\frac{1}{2}$ hours before bedtime for two nights. The next week, the same women took a **lukewarm** bath. The women slept better after the hot baths than after the lukewarm ones.

Ginger Tea for <u>Nausea</u>.

5   **Ginger** can help you feel better if you feel sick to your stomach. It may also help prevent **motion sickness.** Drinking ginger tea is one way to take ginger. To make the tea: Use a small piece of fresh ginger. Take the skin off and cut the ginger into little squares. Put these squares in a cup with a little sugar and add boiling water. Let the tea sit for five minutes before drinking.

An Oatmeal or Baking Soda Bath for <u>Itchy Skin</u>.

6   **Soaking** in an **oatmeal** bath can help **itchy** skin. Put one or two cups of oatmeal in a bathtub filled with warm water. The oatmeal will help stop the itch. If you have insect bites or a **sunburn,** the bath will make you will feel better. **Baking soda** can help **bee stings** to stop hurting. Make a **paste** of baking soda and water and put it on the bee sting.

Acupressure for <u>Headaches</u>.

7   You can cure a headache without drugs. Although no one under-stands how it works, something called *acupressure* seems to help headaches. To practice acupressure, do these things:

- Use your **thumbnail** to apply hard **pressure.** Press into the soft area between your thumb and your first finger.

- Also press above your wrist bone, on the same side as your thumb.

This remedy has been used in Asia for hundreds of years.

8   Although these home remedies work, not all home cures do. If someone tells you a home remedy, be careful. Always ask your doctor if you aren't sure. And if your symptoms continue, be sure to see your doctor.

 **After You Read**

Decide if the following statements are true or false, according to the reading. Write "T" for true and "F" for false.

1. _____ Hot chicken soup is good for colds.

2. _____ A hot bath and a lukewarm bath both help insomnia.

3. _____ Ginger tea can help you if you feel sick to your stomach.

4. _____ Ginger tea can prevent headaches.

5. _____ An oatmeal bath can make itchy skin feel better.

6. _____ Acupressure will help insomnia.

7. _____ It's important to try all home remedies to see if they work.

8. _____ Using pressure can help a headache.

9. _____ Baking soda, oatmeal, and butter are good for skin injuries.

Test-Taking Tip

Understand true-false tests in order to do well on them.

- Be careful of statements that are 95% true. If a statement is even a *little* false, you should mark it false.

- Look at the wording carefully. Statements that include a negative word, such as "not," "never," etc., can sometimes be confusing. Be sure you understand what a "true" or "false" answer means for these statements.

- Look for words like "can" or "might," which usually lead to true answers. "Always" and "never," usually lead to false answers.

◆ Vocabulary Building

Choose the right word to go in the blank.

1. A word for the problem of not being able to sleep is _____.

   a. sickness   c. symptoms

   b. the flu   d. insomnia

2. _____ is good for bee stings.

   a. Chicken soup   c. Insomnia

   b. Baking soda   d. Ginger

3. Taking a _____ bath helps your skin, but not your insomnia.

   a. hot   c. lukewarm

   b. ginger   d. soaking

4. One symptom of motion sickness is _____.

    a. nausea   c. sunburm

    b. itchiness   d. bee stings

5. When you mix water and baking soda, you get _____.

    a. insomnia   c. a headache

    b. a paste   d. itchy

6. If your skin is itchy, you can take _____ bath.

    a. a cold   c. a mixture

    b. a paste   d. an oatmeal

7. Home remedies are not always _____.

    a. effective   c. dangerous

    b. safe   d. a, b, and c

◆ Grammar You Can Use

Giving Advice Using "Should"

Use the modal "should" + the base form of a verb to give advice to someone. For example, if a friend tells you that she has a cold, you could say:

| You | should | drink | hot | liquids. |
| | (modal) | (base form) | | |

Use "should + base form" and write advice for these three health problems.

1. (insomnia) _____

   _____

   _____

2. (itchy skin) _____

   _____

   _____

3. (a cold) _____

   _____

   _____

Role Play

Choose one of these role plays. Work with a partner and practice this role play. Use modals of advice.

1: Asthma

Student A: You think you have asthma and you don't know what to do. Tell your problem to a family member (Student B) and ask for advice.

Student B: You are Student A's family member. Give him/her advice for the asthma.

2: Headache

Student A: You have a headache and you don't know what to do. Tell your problem to a friend (Student B) and ask for advice.

Student B: You are Student A's friend. Give him/her advice for the headache.

LANGUAGE LEARNING STRATEGY

Skim a reading to understand the main idea. Skimming means reading something quickly. Sometimes you don't have time to read carefully. Other times, you may just want to get the main idea of a reading. Skimming is helpful in these cases.

When you skim, you should:

- Keep your eyes moving. Don't stop or reread.

- Read groups of words. Don't stop to think about single words or phrases.

- Have a time limit. Give yourself only a minute or two to skim a short reading, more time for longer readings.

- Make some notes about the main idea.

Apply the Strategy

Skim the next reading. Take only two minutes. Then answer the following questions:

1. What is caffeine? _____

    _____

    _____

2. What are some sources of caffeine? _____

    _____

3. Is caffeine good for you? Why or why not? _____

    _____

Getting Ready to Read

Vocabulary Check

Look at the list of words below. Put a check mark next to the ones you know. Talk with your class about the words you don't know. Write the new words you learn in your Vocabulary Log.

_____ addictive	_____ brewed	_____ on edge
_____ alert	_____ habit-forming	_____ stimulant
_____ behave	_____ instant	_____ tense
_____ bitter	_____ mild	
_____ boost	_____ odorless	

Read

Reading 3: Caffeine

1 Caffeine is a **bitter**-tasting, **odorless** drug found in different kinds of plants. Four sources of caffeine are coffee beans, tea leaves, cocoa beans, and cola nuts. Many products containing caffeine are made from these plants, such as coffee, tea, chocolate, and cola drinks.

2   Caffeine is a **mild stimulant.** It speeds up the way the brain and body work. People say that caffeine gives them a **boost** of energy and makes them more **alert.** They say caffeine helps them think more clearly and work more quickly.

3   Though it is not as harmful as many other drugs, caffeine is not completely safe. Like other drugs, caffeine can hurt the body. Too much caffeine can cause insomnia, headaches, and nausea. Like other drugs, caffeine can change the way people think, feel, and **behave.** Caffeine can make people very **tense** or nervous; they feel "**on edge.**" Caffeine is not as **addictive** as other drugs;

but it is **habit-forming,** and it can be difficult for people to stop taking caffeine once they start taking it regularly.

4   Caffeine is a legal drug, and it is found in many everyday products. Most people do not even think of caffeine as a drug. But it is very easy to get too much of this everyday drug.

Caffeine: How Much Is Too Much?

5 How much caffeine do you use each day? To help you measure how much caffeine you take, here's a chart of some products and the amount of caffeine they contain.

Food or Product:	Caffeine (in milligrams):
Coffee (6 ounces)	
brewed	80–150
instant	40–65
Hot tea (6 ounces)	20–40
Iced tea (12 ounces)	67–76
Soda (12 ounces)	36–54
Chocolate candy (1 ounce)	10–30
Chocolate cake (small slice)	20–30
Chocolate milk (5 ounces)	2–15
Some pain relievers (1 tablet)	32–65

Source: *The Drug Alert Dictionary and Resource Guide,* 1991, Jeffrey Shulman.

After You Read

Answer these questions with your classmates:

1. What are some of the sources of caffeine?

2. Why isn't caffeine "completely safe"?

3. Why do people enjoy caffeine?

4. What health problems can caffeine cause?

5. Why is it difficult to stop taking caffeine?

6. Which food or product contains the most caffeine?

7. Which food or product contains the least caffeine?

8. How much caffeine do some pain relievers contain?

9. What products with caffeine do you enjoy?

10. Do you drink coffee? Have you ever tried to stop?

◆Vocabulary Building

Write the correct word in the blanks below.

boost	on edge	stimulant	odorless	addictive
brewed	mild	alert	bitter	habit-forming

1. Caffeine is a _____ _____ that speeds up your body.

2. Coffee isn't as _____ as other drugs, but it can be

   _____.

3. Asha felt _____ after she had three cups of coffee.

4. _____ coffee has more caffeine than instant does.

5. Many people like caffeine because it helps them feel _____

   —it really gives them a _____.

6. Without sugar, coffee tastes _____.

7. Although coffee smells good, caffeine is _____.

ACADEMIC POWER STRATEGY

Set realistic academic goals. A realistic goal is something that you can realistically expect to accomplish with your skills, time, and hard work. Here are some examples:

Realistic goal: Study English for an hour each night.

Unrealistic goal: Study for four difficult tests in two hours.

Realistic goal: Improve your quiz scores by studying every night.

Unrealistic goal: Always get a perfect grade on every quiz, even if you don't study.

(continued on next page)

It's good to set high goals. But, if you have too many unrealistic ones, you may be frustrated when you don't reach them.

Apply the Strategy

Think of your goals for this English course. Write three of them here:

1. _____

_____

_____

2. _____

_____

_____

3. _____

_____

_____

Review these goals. Are they realistic or unrealistic? If any of them is unrealistic, rewrite it to make it more realistic. Write your revised goal here.

_____

_____

_____

TUNING IN: "Stress Depression"

Before you watch "Stress Depression," look at the following list of words and phrases. Put a check mark next to the ones you know. Discuss with your class the words and phrases you don't know. Write the new words and phrases you learn in your Vocabulary Log.

© CNN

_____ ally   _____ clinical

_____ anxious   _____ flex time

_____ blue-collar job   _____ hostile

_____ productivity   _____ working woman

_____ white-collar job   _____ workplace

Now watch the video. What are some of the jobs that the women in the video are doing? Write down the jobs you see.

_____

_____

_____

Watch the video again and answer these questions:

1. What two things cause stress in the workplace?

2. What happens to people because of stress?

3. How do men behave when they experience workplace stress?

4. What advice does Madeline Woolright, a psychologist in the video, give to women about workplace stress?

PUTTING IT ALL TOGETHER

Read the Heart Disease Risk Chart. Circle the number that applies to you in each question.

> The human heart is about the size of a fist and weights about 250–350 grams (9 ounces).

Heart Disease Risk Chart					
1. Sex	1	Female under 40	5	Male	
	2	Female 40–50	6	Heavy male	
	3	Female 50+			
2. Age	1	10–20	4	41–50	
	2	21–30	5	51–60	
	3	31–40	8	61+	
3. Weight	0	5 pounds underweight	3	21–35 pounds overweight	
	1	5 pounds overweight	5	36–50 pounds overweight	
	2	6–20 pounds overweight	7	50+ pounds overweight	

Heart Disease Risk Chart *(continued)*

4.	Smoking	0	don't smoke		
		1	only smoke cigars or pipes		
		2	smoke 10 cigarettes or less each day		
		4	smoke 10–20 cigarettes each day		
		6	smoke 20–40 cigarettes each day		
		10	smoke more than 40 cigarettes a day		
5.	Exercise	1	a lot	6	very little
		2	some	8	none
6.	Fatty Foods	1	Don't eat animal fat	4	Eat about 30% animal fat
		2	Eat about 10% animal fat	5	Eat about 40% animal fat
		3	Eat about 20% animal fat	7	Eat more than 50% animal fat

SCORES

Add up the numbers you circled. Write the total here: _____

Here is what your total score means:

5–10   Below average risk for heart disease

11–24   Average risk for heart disease

25–30   Above average risk for heart disease

31–40   High risk for heart disease

> 46 million Americans smoke. 400,000 deaths each year are related to smoking. 16 million Americans attempt to quit smoking each year but fewer than 10% of smokers who to try to quit each year succeed.
>
> **—DRAKE UNIVERSITY ONLINE**

1. What habits do you think you should change?

2. What can you do to decrease your risk of heart disease? Write some realistic goals.

3. Write a short paragraph giving yourself some advice. Use the correct *modal* form (see page 51).

CHECK YOUR PROGRESS

On a scale of 1 to 5, rate how well you've mastered the goals set at the beginning of the chapter:

1 2 3 4 5   find examples in your reading.

1 2 3 4 5   skim to get the main idea.

1 2 3 4 5   set realistic academic goals.

1 2 3 4 5   do well on true-false tests.

1 2 3 4 5   use correct grammar when you give advice.

If you've given yourself a 3 or lower on any of these goals:

- visit the *Tapestry* web site for additional practice.
- ask your instructor for extra help.
- review the sections of the chapter that you found difficult.
- work with a partner or study group to further your progress.

L ook at the photos. Then discuss these questions with your class:

- Do you think people damage the environment? How?
- What should we do with all our garbage?
- What is an endangered species?
- Should people hunt and fish?

ONLY ONE EARTH

The world's population is growing. And, as it grows, people use more resources and throw away more garbage. Many people worry about this problem. They try to use less, re-use more, and help make laws to protect the earth. However, other people are more concerned about jobs and food. They may need to fish or cut trees to live. This chapter looks at these ideas.

Setting Goals

In this chapter, you will learn how to:

◆ use background knowledge.

◆ find topic sentences.

◆ practice what you learn.

◆ get better organized for tests.

◆ understand prepositions better.

Which goal is most important to you? _____

_____

Why? _____

Talk about your answers with your class.

◆ Getting Started

Which problem is the biggest in the world? Ask five people to rank these five problems from "1" for most important to "5" for least important. If you don't know some of the words here, talk about them with your class before you begin and add them to your Vocabulary Log.

Problem	Person 1	Person 2	Person 3	Person 4	Person 5
too much garbage					
endangered animal species					
pollution					
not enough food					
not enough jobs					

After you get answers from five people, compare them with your classmates' answers. Answer these questions:

1. Which problem seems most important to people?
2. Which problem is the least important?
3. Do you agree with these rankings?
4. Why or why not?

◆ Getting Ready to Read

> After one look at this planet any visitor from outer space would say, "I want to see the manager."
>
> —WILLIAM BURROUGHS

Vocabulary Check

Look at the words and phrases below. Put a check mark next to the ones that you know. Talk with your class about the words and phrases you don't know. Write the new words you learn in your Vocabulary Log.

_____ control	_____ frozen	_____ nets
_____ dim	_____ given up	_____ satellites
_____ engines	_____ ignored	_____ threatens
_____ estimate (verb)	_____ illegal	_____ tons
_____ fault	_____ market	_____ wasteful

Vocabulary Note: _tuna, cod, haddock,_ and _sablefish_ are types of fish.

LANGUAGE LEARNING STRATEGY

Use your background knowledge to help you understand a reading. Your background knowledge can help you become a better reader. To discover what you know about a subject, write down the topic that you are going to read about. Then write down all related words, phrases, and ideas you can think of. Don't worry about grammar or spelling.

Apply the Strategy

What do you know about fishing? Explore your background knowledge about this subject by doing the following activity. Write down everything you know about fishing. Include names of fish, ways of fishing, and anything else you know about the subject of fish and fishing. Remember, don't worry about grammar and spelling.

> Fishing

 Read

Reading 1: Give a Man a Fish

1 There is an old saying: "Give a man a fish; you have fed him for today. Teach a man to fish, and you have fed him for a lifetime." However, today, this saying may no longer be true. The reason is overfishing.

2 The boats in the Maricaban Strait of the Philippines **dim** their lights and bring in their **nets.** Fishing with lights is **illegal** in the Philippines, but the law is often **ignored,** as it is a better way to catch fish. Fish are becoming very hard to catch in the South China Sea.

3 The boats take their fish to **market** twenty minutes away. There, you can buy fresh **tuna,** along with many other kinds of

fish. The market, which opens at 6:30 each morning, used to stay open until 10:00 or 11:00. Now the fish are gone by 8:00. Many of the fish are very small. Some are types people don't enjoy eating much. One trader has **given up** fish and sells chicken instead.

4   It is clear that overfishing affects poor countries like the Philippines. But it also affects rich countries. Even though rich countries have enough money to help solve the problem, the fish are disappearing from these areas as well. An area of New England and Canada called the Grand Banks once had excellent fishing. In the 1960s, fishermen caught 1.6 million **tons** of **cod** there. Thirty years later, they only caught 22,000 tons. Canada finally had to close the Grand Banks. 40,000 jobs were lost.

5   The effects of overfishing are hidden by statistics. Some reports show that the world's supply of fish is still growing, even though people fish more. But these reports do not report on the *type* of fish that are increasing in supply. This can hide the fact that some types of fish are disappearing.

6   Overfishing **threatens** every waterway. As a result, the world supply of cod and **haddock,** a favorite fish to eat, has not grown since the early 1970s. Some countries have tried to **control** fishing for over 100 years, but it hasn't helped.

7   The problem of overfishing is spreading. Since anyone can fish, many people do. Around the world, the number of fishermen and fish farmers is growing. The total has more than doubled in the past 25 years.

8   When too many people fish, too many fish are caught. In Alaska in the early 1990s, anyone could catch **sablefish,** although the total amount was controlled. As a result, a year's worth of

sablefish was caught in less than one week. Fish that aren't eaten immediately must be frozen. Since people pay less for **frozen** fish than fresh, this kind of fishing is **wasteful.**

9　　But overfishing isn't the **fault** of just the fishermen. Governments pay people to fish. A new study by the World Bank says that these payments are worth about $16 billion a year.

10　　Open waters and government pay lead to too many fishermen. Canadian scientists **estimate** that 53% of the world's boats are not needed. Nevertheless, some countries are still increasing their fishing industries. The number of Chinese fishermen doubled twice between 1970 and 1990. Chinese officials say they want it to grow more. The European Union is fishing in Africa because there are too many fishermen in Europe. Morocco and Namibia tried to end European fishing in the 1990s, but they were not successful. When Europe sold its extra boats in South America, the boats were used to overfish in Argentina.

11　　Finally, there is another cause of overfishing: better technology. Many poor countries do not have large boats for fishing. However, the rich countries bring their boats to those countries. These boats have new **engines, satellites,** and computers. And, the technology improves all the time. Better technology makes it easier to catch more fish.

12　　Unfortunately, the days of teaching people to fish may be over. There are too many fishermen and too many fish being caught. New solutions to this problem must be found, before there are no more fish to eat.

◆**After You Read**

1. What does the "old saying" in the first paragraph mean?

2. Why may this saying not be true any longer?

3. Why do Philippine fishermen use lights to fish?

4. What has happened to the fish market in the Philippines?

5. Where are the Grand Banks?

6. How do statistics hide overfishing facts?

7. How is overfishing spreading?

8. Why is it wasteful to catch too many fish too quickly?

9. Whose fault is overfishing?

10. Why is the European Union fishing in Africa?

11. How did European Union boats affect fishing in South America?

12. How does technology affect fishing?

74% less air pollution and 35% less water pollution occurs when paper is made from recycled materials.

◆Vocabulary Building

Complete the sentences, showing you understand the words in bold.

1. It is **wasteful** to _____.
2. Three things you find in a **market** are _____, _____, and _____.
3. _____ **threatens** the environment.
4. Please **dim** the _____.
5. I **estimate** there are _____ in my school.
6. Overfishing is _____ **fault**.
7. _____ is **illegal**.
8. I have **given up** _____.
9. We should not **ignore** _____.

◆Getting Ready to Read

Some people in cold climates like to wear fur. Fur keeps people very warm. However, many people believe wearing fur is wrong. They think animals should not be killed just to make clothing. What do you think? Discuss these questions with your class:

1. Do many people in your native culture wear fur?
2. Should people wear fur? Why or why not?
3. If you lived in a really cold climate, would you wear fur? Why or why not?

Vocabulary Check

Look at the words and phrases below. Put a check mark next to the ones that you know. Talk with your class about the words and phrases you don't know. Write the new words you learn in your Vocabulary Log.

____ beavers	____ foxes	____ nuisance
____ contracted	____ gopher	____ prey
____ dammed	____ impressive	____ raccoons
____ demand (noun)	____ in the long run	____ season
____ ditches	____ lack	____ skinning
____ drawbacks	____ make a good living	____ starve
____ environmentalists	____ mink	____ trappers

Read

Reading 2: A Trapper's Life

1 Trapping used to be a way to **make a good living.** That has certainly changed over the past several years. The **demand** for furs is nearly gone. **Environmentalists** think trapping is wrong. However, for 24-year-old Johnny Martin, trapping remains a way of life.

2 Martin started trapping when he was 9. He saw some traps hanging in his parents' garage and decided to set them out around his house. He hoped to trap a few rabbits.

3 Rabbits aren't the trapper's most valuable **prey,** but Martin enjoyed his first trapping experience. It developed into a lifelong love.

4 Martin is one of the last full-time **trappers** in Wisconsin. He has more than 700 traps. He drives about 160 miles a day and collects animals on about 150 farms in central Wisconsin. He makes a pretty good living. He traps enough animals to make up for low fur prices.

5 "For me, quantity is more important than quality," he said. "I can make up for the low fur prices by bringing in more than the average trapper."

6 The number of animals his traps catch is truly **impressive.** Last year, he trapped more than 100 **mink,** 150 **raccoons,** 300 **foxes,** and hundreds of other small animals.

7 Farmers also hire Martin to trap **nuisance** animals. He receives two dollars for each **gopher** he traps. Last year, he trapped nearly 10,000 gophers. He earns about $20,000 a year on gopher trapping alone.

8 The Department of Natural Resources also has **contracted** with Martin. About twelve times a year, he traps **beavers** that have **dammed ditches** or flooded private land.

9 Trapping full-time does have its **drawbacks,** however. For example, his home is filled with animal skins. It's also hard for him to take a day off. State law requires that traps be checked every day.

10 "It can be very hard work," Martin said. "My day usually starts before the sun rises, and it lasts until after dark. Then, I spend the rest of the evening **skinning** animals and preparing for the next day. I really don't get a day off during trapping **season.**"

11 As a full-time trapper, Martin worries about the views people have of his profession. He thinks that most anti-trapping groups don't understand that trapping animals helps **in the long run.**

12 "Most of these people don't know how animals live. They don't understand the animals' environment," he said. "Overpopulation is a big problem. I've seen animals **starve.** There is also lots of disease when there are too many animals in one area.

13 "There are areas where I can't trap right now. Most of the animals in those areas are sick with disease, because of the **lack** of food and overpopulation. I'd like to show anyone who is against trapping some of the terrible things I've seen."

◆After You Read

1. What is trapping?

2. How has trapping changed over the past several years?

3. What kinds of animals does Mr. Martin trap?

4. What are the drawbacks of being a trapper?

5. What is an example of a nuisance animal?

6. Why does Mr. Martin trap beavers?

7. What is Mr. Martin's day like?

8. Why doesn't Mr. Martin agree with anti-trapping groups?

9. Do you agree with Mr. Martin? Why or why not?

◆Vocabulary Building

"A Trapper's Life" had many names of animals in it. Can you match the animal with its picture? Work with a partner. Write the animal's name below the correct picture.

beaver   gopher   mink   raccoon   rabbit

1. _____   2. _____   3. _____   4. _____   5. _____

◆Grammar You Can Use

Idioms with Prepositions

Prepositions, words such as *in, on, from,* and *at,* can be confusing, especially when they are used in idioms and take on a special meaning. Here are some of the idioms that use prepositions from "A Trapper's Life":

Make <u>up for</u> something
Take/Get a day <u>off</u>
<u>In</u> the long run

Certain words are often used with certain prepositions. Here are more examples from the reading:

The <u>demand</u> *for* something
To <u>set</u> something *out*
To <u>develop</u> *into* something
To be <u>filled</u> *with* something
To <u>prepare</u> *for* something
To <u>worry</u> *about* something

The best way to remember these phrases is to write them down and use them in your writing and speaking. Add these words and phrases to your Vocabulary Log. Write a sentence for each of them, too.

Test-Taking Tip

Get organized before you take a test. When you are organized, you can focus on studying. When you can't find your notes, your books, or your old assignments, you waste studying time.

Here's how to get organized:

- Make sure all your notes, assignments, and old tests are in a notebook, organized by date.

- Put all your books and notebooks for your classes in one place. You can find everything easily this way.

- Write down the phone numbers and e-mail addresses of friends you can study with.

- Put studying time on your schedule.

When you are organized, you will feel more confident about taking tests.

◆ **Getting Ready to Read**

Skim this reading. Take only 2 minutes. After you skim, answer these questions:

1. What is the main idea of the reading? _____

_____

2. What is *extinction*? _____

_____

3. What is the Endangered Species Act? _____

_____

Talk about your answers before you read more carefully.

Vocabulary Check

Look at the words and phrases below. Put a check mark next to the ones that you know. Talk with your class about the words and phrases you don't know. Write the new words you learn in your Vocabulary Log.

_____ appeal (verb)	_____ grizzly bears	_____ snails
_____ aware	_____ ignorance	_____ spotted owls
_____ clams	_____ interfere	_____ treasures
_____ delicate	_____ loggers	_____ tropical
_____ endangered	_____ mussels	_____ wolves
_____ extinct	_____ rubber	

> In 1900 there were 100,000 tigers in the world, and today there are fewer than 6,000.
>
> —ENN DAILY NEWS

Read

Reading 3: Going, Going, Gone

1 Earth's animals are disappearing faster than they reproduce. Because there is too little research and too much **ignorance,** no one is **aware** of how much we are losing.

2   Many different kinds of plants and animals are becoming **extinct.** Every year, one-half of one percent of the living things in the **tropical** rain forests become extinct. Some disappear before they are found and named. No one has time to study them before they are gone.

3   The disappearance of species worries scientists and environmentalists. They want the U.S. Endangered Species Act of 1973 to be made stronger. This act was formed to protect endangered species. However, **loggers,** land developers, and factory owners disagree. They want changes that will make the act weaker. They think the act is not working. They believe it is not fair to private landowners. They want the act to consider people more. Environmentalists worry about our disappearing resources and loggers worry about jobs.

4   Environmentalists think the Endangered Species Act is an important tool. It uses laws to protect animals and plants. It keeps the developers off of **delicate** land. It slows the cutting of old forests. And, it protects **endangered** species.

5   Today, 740 different living things are listed as either threatened or endangered. Another 400 species are waiting to be added to the list. However, some of those 400 species have become extinct while waiting.

6   Therefore, environmentalists are working to strengthen the act. At the same time, loggers, developers, and farmers are working to weaken it. They don't want the **spotted owls, grizzly bears,** or **wolves** to be protected. The loggers think owls **interfere** with logging jobs. Farmers don't want bears and wolves protected, since they attack other animals.

7   But many people think the act has been effective in many ways. It has not only protected animals, but it has changed the behavior of private and public land users.

8   As the fight continues, however, almost everyone agrees that some of the numbers are bad. The rivers and streams of America are in danger. The nation's fresh water faces large losses. The rivers and lakes were once home to many kinds of **snails, mussels,** and **clams.** The freshwater mussels of North America include 247 kinds: 13 are extinct, 40 are endangered, 2 are threatened, and 74 more might become endangered.

9   Some environmentalists try to **appeal** to businesses. They say that studying unknown plants may be a good business idea. Plants give us important materials: drugs, **rubber,** food, and other products come from trees and plants.

10   Nature's **treasures** are disappearing before we know about them. The cure for cancer or AIDS may be hiding in the rain forest. With such riches, many believe, we must save the environment to save ourselves.

◆ After You Read

1. How many living things in the tropical rain forest are becoming extinct each year?

2. What is the Endangered Species Act?

3. Why do environmentalists want to make the Act stronger?

4. Why do loggers and farmers want to make the Act weaker?

5. Why don't some people want to protect spotted owls or wolves?

6. How do environmentalists try to appeal to business?

7. How might the rain forest help people?

8. Which is more important: jobs or the environment? Why?

LANGUAGE LEARNING STRATEGY

Find the topic sentences of paragraphs to understand the main ideas. Most paragraphs have topic sentences—sentences that tell the main idea of the paragraph. Look at these two paragraphs from "Going, Going, Gone":

> As the fight continues, however, almost everyone agrees that some of the numbers are bad. *The rivers and streams of America are in danger.* The nation's fresh water faces large losses. The rivers and lakes were once home to many kinds of snails, mussels, and clams. The freshwater mussels of North America include 247 kinds: 13 are extinct, 40 are endangered, 2 are threatened, and 74 more might become endangered.
>
> *Some environmentalists try to appeal to businesses.* They say that studying unknown plants may be a good business idea. Plants give us important materials: drugs, rubber, food, and other products come from trees and plants.

The topic sentence is in italics in each of the two paragraphs above. Most of the information in each paragraph relates to the topic sentence. Understanding topic sentences will help you read faster. You will know the main ideas before you read the examples.

Apply the Strategy

Reread "Going, Going, Gone." Underline the topic sentence in each paragraph. Work with a partner. Then talk about your answers with your class.

Vocabulary Building

In the past 200 years, the United States has lost 50 percent of its wetlands, 90 percent of its northwestern old-growth forests, 99 percent of its tall grass prairie, and up to 490 species of native plants and animals.

—ENN DAILY NEWS

Match the word in column A with its meaning in column B. Draw a line to the correct answer.

Column A	Column B
1. at risk	a. delicate
2. no longer living	b. loggers
3. related to the tropics	c. treasures
4. lumberjacks	d. extinct
5. mindful	e. appeals
6. requests	f. tropical
7 riches	g. interfere
8. stupidity	h. aware
9. be in the way	i. ignorance
10. tender	j. endangered

ACADEMIC POWER STRATEGY

Apply the Strategy

Practice what you learn to connect your readings with your life. You can practice what you learn in many ways. If you are reading about math, do some math problems to practice the skills you have read about. If you are reading some advice, you can practice following the advice in your own life. Practicing what you are learning will help you remember information and will make reading a valuable experience.

Review the readings in this chapter. Write three ways that you could connect your reading with your life:

EXAMPLE: *Visit a fish market to learn the English names of fish.*

1. _____

2. _____

3. _____

Getting Ready to Read

Before you read "Down in the Dumps" about the problem of too much garbage, watch the CNN video, "Garbage School."

TUNING IN: "Garbage School"

Before you watch the video "Garbage School," look at the list of words below. Put a check mark next to the words you know. With your teacher and your class, discuss the words you don't know. Write the new words you learn in your Vocabulary Log.

———— cozy   ———— methane gas   ———— pungent

———— decomposing   ———— partnership   ———— skeptical

———— landfill   ———— proximity   ———— thermostat

Watch the video. Circle the items below that you see in the video.

students playing instruments   burning garbage   garbage

students playing sports   garbage trucks   a fire

students throwing away trash   pipes   a thermostat

students at computers

Watch the video again and answer these questions:

1. What is the name of the high school in the video?

2. Where is the high school located?

3. How far is it from the landfill?

4. How does the landfill help the high school?

5. Whose idea was it to use the landfill to help the high school?

Vocabulary Check

Look at the words below. Put a check mark next to the words that you know. Talk with your class about the words you don't know. Write the new words you learn in your Vocabulary Log.

———— aluminum   ———— gases   ———— surrounds

———— blessing   ———— goods   ———— transformed

———— depth   ———— loads   ———— tractors

———— drill   ———— pyramid

———— feast   ———— sealed

© CNN

Read

Reading 4: Down In the Dumps

1   The Hiriya garbage dump covers more than 405 hectares.[1] There is nothing but plastic bags, paper, and every other kind of trash. A high dirt wall **surrounds** the whole area.

2   In one corner, garbage trucks line up to dump their **loads.** From just one morning, the garbage has grown into a **pyramid** about six meters high.

3   With tons of garbage, the smell is terrible, but you get used to it in a couple of minutes. The top of Hiriya is very high, and the wind carries the smell. About ten workers are walking about the edges of the garbage, picking up **aluminum** and boxes for re-use.

4   Thousands of birds, which come to Hiriya every February and November, are having a **feast.**

5   "Hiriya is a **blessing.** You can make a living here for the rest of your life," says a worker who collects aluminum.

6   Another worker is less thankful. He explains, using an old Arab saying: "For me it's not one day honey, one day onions, but more like one day honey, three days onions."

7   Eleven cities take their garbage to Hiriya, adding 3,250 tons per day. That makes over one million tons a year. It is the biggest garbage dump in the Middle East. There are bigger ones, however, in Europe and the United States. For example, the Staten Island, New York, dump collects twice as much garbage as Hiriya does.

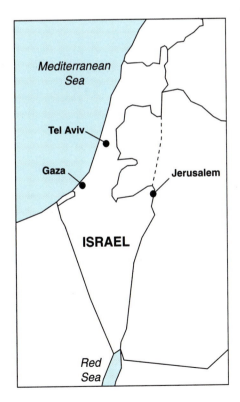

8   The growth of Hiriya shows the growth in the number of **goods** people in Israel are using.

9   Hundreds of thousands of drivers pass Hiriya every day, but most probably don't notice it. It is near Tel Aviv, surrounded by trees and vegetable fields. It looks like a big hill, not a mountain of garbage.

[1]A hectare is about 2 acres.

10   However, nobody wants Hiriya to continue as a garbage dump. Since opening in 1951, it has grown into an ugly brown mountain in the middle of the country. Rivers of sewage run along the sides of the dump. They pick up liquid waste that has soaked into the earth. Passing Hiriya, these dirty rivers continue into a pipe and finally go to a sewage treatment plant.

11   Hiriya is running out of room. Each year, it rises higher. On the ground, the dump measures a hundred hectares; on the top, thirty. Soon, there will be no more room at the top. People hope it closes before long.

12   But what do you do with 40 million tons of garbage and dirt? And what about all the **gases** and liquids that are inside the mountain? You can't move Hiriya. So, the plan is to turn the Middle East's biggest garbage dump into a park.

13   First it will be covered with more earth. Next, they'll **drill** holes into it and collect the gas. Then it will be **sealed** with plastic. Finally, it will be covered with more soil. Afterward, grass, trees and flowers will be planted.

14   But before Hiriya can be **transformed** into a park, the cities in the area must find a different place to put their garbage. The new dump will be a modern landfill: the liquids will be taken out and the gases will be collected. It will be completely covered and sealed at the bottom. At Hiriya, there's none of this. It's an environmental disaster.

15   For now, however, Hiriya Park is still a dream. It will be very expensive to make the dump a place a family can enjoy. It won't be done for 10 or 20 years.

16   So the trucks keep driving to the top of the garbage mountain, where they pile the garbage higher. They dump it in one corner; **tractors** spread and flatten a couple of days' trash to a **depth** of about three meters; other trucks put about a half-meter of dirt over it. Then the process begins again in another spot. When one whole section is filled, they move onto the next section. The garbage just gets deeper.

After You Read

1. Where is Hiriya?

2. How big is the garbage dump there?

3. How old is the garbage dump?

4. Why do some workers like the garbage dump?

5. Why do some workers dislike the garbage dump?

6. Where are the biggest garbage dumps in the world?

7. Why is the garbage dump in Hiriya growing?

8. Why don't drivers notice the Hiriya dump?

9. What is the future of the Hiriya dump?

10. Why can't they move Hiriya?

11. What will the new garbage dump be like?

12. Would you like to visit Hiriya Park when they finish it? Why or why not?

◄Vocabulary Building

Write the correct word in the blanks.

aluminum	feast	sealed
blessing	gases	surrounds
depth	loads	tractors
drill	pyramid	

1. Some workers think the Hiriya dump is a _____.
   They collect _____
   to sell.

2. The trucks bring in many _____
   of garbage every day, and the _____
   spread the garbage out.

3. A dirt wall _____
   the Hiriya garbage dump. The garbage reaches a
   _____ of three meters.

4. They need to _____ holes to
   release some of the _____ in
   the garbage.

5. The garbage is piled up into a _____.

6. The Hiriya dump is not _____
   at the bottom, but the new dump will be.

7. The birds have a _____
   on the food they find at the dump.

PUTTING IT ALL TOGETHER

Read the description of the town of Whitewater:

Whitewater is a beautiful small town in the mountains. There is a beautiful lake and a lot of wild animals. People enjoy swimming, fishing, and boating. Some people make a living from small farms. Others have businesses that appeal to tourists. Everyone treasures their beautiful environment, but some can't agree how to use it best.

In a group, assign these roles:

- Cynthia Chung, a scientist. She has found that the lake is becoming polluted, and fish are dying.
- Howard and Barbara Jackson, local farmers. They don't believe their farm is polluting the lake. They say there are too many boats and fishermen on the lake.
- Susana Morales, an environmentalist. She wants the lake cleaned up. She wants people to stop fishing and boating there until they're sure it's safe. She also thinks the Jacksons should stop using chemicals on their farm.
- Jack Thomas, a fisherman and tour operator. He is concerned that a polluted lake will ruin fishing and hurt the tourist business.
- Sally Mason, the mayor of Whitewater. She wants to find a solution to the problem.
- Pat Hahn, the local newspaper reporter, who wants to write about this story.

Read the descriptions carefully. Then each person should explain their ideas. Talk about the problem, and reach a solution. Help Pat Hahn write his story about the problem.

CHECK YOUR PROGRESS

On a scale of 1 to 5, rate how well you've mastered the goals set at the beginning of the chapter:

1 2 3 4 5   use background knowledge.

1 2 3 4 5   find topic sentences.

1 2 3 4 5   practice what you learn.

1 2 3 4 5   get better organized for tests.

1 2 3 4 5   understand prepositions better.

If you've given yourself a 3 or lower on any of these goals:

- visit the *Tapestry* web site for additional practice.
- ask your instructor for extra help.
- review the sections of the chapter that you found difficult.
- work with a partner or study group to further your progress.

Look at the photo. Then discuss these questions with your class:

- Have you ever traveled by train? Did you enjoy it?
- Do you prefer airplanes or trains? Why?
- Do you like to drive? Why or why not?

TRAINS, PLANES, AND AUTOMOBILES

How do people get from place to place? Often, the answer depends on many things: how far people have to go, how long the trip will take, how expensive it will be, and how comfortable the trip is. This chapter gives information about different kinds of transportation such as trains, bicycles, cars, and airplanes.

Setting Goals

In this chapter, you will learn how to:

◆ use a graphic organizer.

◆ study in a group.

◆ use quotations.

◆ make a time line.

◆ use flash cards to study for tests.

Which goal is most important to you?_____

_____

Why?_____

Talk about your answers with your class.

◆**Getting Started**

1. Before you begin this chapter, read the questions in the chart below. With your class, talk about any words you do not understand. Then ask three classmates these questions. Write their answers in the chart.

	Student 1	Student 2	Student 3
1. How do you get to school each day?			
2. What kind of transportation do you use when you go on longer trips?			
3. Have you ever been on an airplane?			
4. If so, did you like it? If not, would you like to?			

After you complete the chart, talk about these questions:

- How do most of your classmates get to school?
- How do your classmates travel on longer trips?
- How many of your classmates like to fly?

2. Preview this chapter. Answer these questions:

a. Which reading has the most interesting title?

_____

b. Which reading topics do you know something about already?

_____

_____

◆**Getting Ready to Read**

Think about all of the places you go each day. Could you go to any of these places by bicycle? Complete the information in the chart. Discuss your answers with your class.

Place you go	Could you ride a bike there?		Why or why not?
1.	Yes	No	
2.	Yes	No	
3.	Yes	No	
4.	Yes	No	

Vocabulary Check

Look at the words and phrases below. Put a check mark next to the ones that you know. Talk with your class about the words and phrases you don't know. Write the new words you learn in your Vocabulary Log.

_____ available	_____ in good shape	_____ rider
_____ bike lanes	_____ mayor	_____ theft
_____ helmet	_____ provide	_____ traffic

 Vocabulary Building

While you read "Free Bike Programs," highlight the words and phrases you learned from the list above. Then look at the sentence the word or phrase is in. Do you understand the word and the sentence? Discuss the sentences you do not understand with your classmates.

Read

The Italian artist and inventor Leonardo da Vinci designed a kind of bicycle five hundred years ago.

Reading 1: Free Bike Programs

1   San Francisco is going to do what many other cities have already done—provide free bicycles to the public. The mayor of San Francisco supports the bicycle program. He wants to improve the terrible traffic problems in the city.

2   At first, 40 to 60 bikes will be available only to city workers. People will give their old bikes to the city to use in the program. If this program is successful, one day more than 1,000 bicycles will be available. Everyone, not just city workers, will be able to use these bicycles.

3   People in Fresno, California already have a free bicycle program. In fact, this idea began in Amsterdam over 40 years ago.

These programs encourage citizens to get out of their cars and onto pollution-free bikes.

4   Fresno's Yellow Bike Program puts about forty bicycles around the city. The bikes are painted bright yellow so people know they can take them. When people take a yellow bike, they can ride to work or to shopping areas, and then leave the bike for the next rider.

5   Some people worry that the free bikes will be stolen. However, theft hasn't been a problem in other free-bike cities.

6   While most people think the bike program is a good idea, only a few say they will use it. "I will still drive my car," says Joanna Greene. "San Francisco has a lot of hills. My office is at the top of Potrero Hill. I don't think I'm in good shape. And, wouldn't I have to carry a helmet with me all the time?"

7   Phil Chung agrees, "There is too much traffic. Riding a bicycle can be dangerous. There are not very many bike lanes." He continues, "Plus, it's too cold in the winter. And what if you ride a bike to work, and then there isn't one to ride home?"

8   Program leaders know there will be problems. But they think it's worth trying. "It's not the solution for everyone," states Sylvia Pass. "But if just one hundred people use it every day, that's one hundred cars that aren't on the streets, one hundred parking spaces that aren't used. I think it's a great beginning."

After You Read

Answer these questions about the free bike programs:

1. How many bicycles will the San Francisco program start with?

2. Why does the mayor support the free bike program?

3. What city had the first bike program?

4. How many bikes does the Fresno Yellow Bike Program have?

5. How do people use the Yellow Bike Program?

6. What are the disadvantages of the free bike program in San Francisco?

7. Why does Sylvia Pass think the program is a good idea?

8. Do you think your city should start a Yellow Bike Program? Why or why not?

Grammar You Can Use

Quotations

In "Free Bike Programs" there are three **quotations.** Quotations tell exactly what someone said. For example:

"I will still drive my car," says Joanna Greene. "San Francisco has a lot of hills."

The words that Joanna Greene spoke are in quotation marks (" "). There is a comma after the quotation and before the main verb in the first sentence. The comma is inside the quotation marks.

In the second sentence, the period comes before the quotation mark.

It is also possible for a quotation to follow the main verb of a sentence. In this case, the main verb is followed by the comma and then the quotation.

Joanna Greene says, "I will still drive my car."

Find and copy two quotations from the article here. Pay close attention to the punctuation.

1. _____

_____

_____

2. _____

_____

_____

Test-Taking Tip

Use flash cards to study for a test. They are an easy and inexpensive tool for studying. Here's how to make and use them:

- Buy some index cards.

- Think about the important words and ideas for the test.

- Write a question on one side of each card and the answer on the back.

- Use the cards to ask yourself or a study partner questions.

- When you know an answer really well, take the card out of the stack. Keep studying the ones you don't know as well.

- Take them with you anyplace where you'll have a little free time. Test yourself during this free time.

Using flash cards can help you remember and understand the things you study.

◆**Getting Ready to Read**

The next reading, "The Fast Track," is about high-speed trains. Some of these trains can go 200 miles per hour. Here are the speeds of other types of transportation. If you are used to the metric system, you might not know how fast these speeds are.

Can you guess which is the fastest? Match the type of transportation with its speed. Draw a line from the type of transportation to its speed. If you want, you can do the math to find out how fast it goes in kilometers per hour. 1 mile = 1.6093 kilometers.

Type of Transportation	Miles Per Hour	Kilometers Per Hour
American high-speed train	25–65	
Automobile	125	
Bicycle	500	
Japanese high-speed train	5–30	
Jet airplane	70	
Military airplane	2000	
Person running	200	
Regular train	3–8	

Vocabulary Check

Look at the words and phrases below. Put a check mark next to the ones you know. Talk with your class about the words and phrases you don't know. Write the new words you learn in your Vocabulary Log.

_____ benches   _____ knocked over   _____ raced

_____ bullet   _____ miles per hour   _____ service

_____ curves   _____ nonstop   _____ stations

_____ exact   _____ passengers   _____ straighter

_____ force   _____ platform   _____ track

_____ governor   _____ prevent

Read

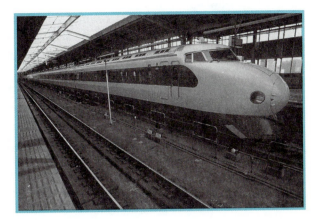

Reading 2: The Fast Track

1 The **passengers** stood on the **platform** waiting for a train back to Tokyo. They were almost **knocked over** by the **force** passing them just a few feet away. What was it? It was a **nonstop** *shinkansen,* or Japanese **bullet** train. It roared through the station going more than 100 **miles per hour.** These trains sometimes go as fast as 200 miles per hour.

2 Before the *shinkansen* passed, the station was quiet. Students sat on **benches** reading books. Men drank coffee and read newspapers. Then the station began to shake. The train **raced** by. When it was gone, everything was quiet again.

3 The word *shinkansen* means "new **track,**" for the special tracks that carry the trains. Every day, millions of people use the bullet trains to travel between Japan's large cities. Millions more travel using the regular trains. The Japanese trains are clean, comfortable, and they are almost always on time.

4 Train travel in the United States is often a less happy experience. Riders complain that the cars are dirty, the **service** is bad, and the trains are often late.

5 In fact, many people wonder why American trains aren't like Japanese ones. Some say that the United States is not like Japan. The United States is very large, and the people live far apart. Americans like cars, and traveling by road. Nonetheless, Amtrak, the American train system, hopes to build a high-speed train in the U.S. This new train, called the *Acela,* will offer service between New York City and other cities on the East Coast of the United States.

6 Amtrak doesn't have an **exact** date for the new service. It believes it will be available at the end of 1999. The new service will cost $2 billion. The costs include new rails, making **curves straighter,** and improving **stations.**

7   "There's no reason America needs to be behind Europe or behind Japan," said Michael Dukakis, the former **governor** of Massachusetts. Mr. Dukakis now works for Amtrak.

8   The new train is not as fast as the bullet trains in other countries. U.S. safety rules **prevent** Amtrak trains from going as fast as some Japanese trains. In fact, Acela service from New York to Washington is only 15 to 30 minutes faster than the regular train. However, the travel time between Boston and New York will be three hours with the new service. The regular train takes four and a half hours.

9   All of Amtrak's new trains will go at least 125 miles per hour, and some will travel as fast as 150 miles per hour. The company will continue to improve its tracks and stations. One day, the trip from New York to Washington may take only two hours, instead of four or five. The new trains will be more comfortable, offer more room, and have better food, too.

10   After the Acela service begins, Amtrak hopes to start high-speed service in five other areas: California, the Midwest, the Pacific Northwest, the Southeast, and the Gulf Coast.

11   Amtrak hopes that Americans will start riding trains again. The company thinks the new service will be very popular. However, some people think train travel will never be popular again in the United States. It is hard to get Americans out of their cars.

 **After You Read**

1. What is a *shinkansen?*

2. How fast does the *shinkansen* go?

3. What does *shinkansen* mean?

4. What are Japanese trains like?

5. What are American trains like?

6. Why aren't American trains like Japanese trains, according to some people?

7. What is the *Acela* service?

8. Where will the *Acela* service be available?

9. What other areas might get high-speed train service in the future?

10. Is the *Acela* faster than the regular trains? How much faster?

11. How fast will the new American trains go? Why won't they go faster?

12. Do you think the service will be popular? Why or why not?

◇Vocabulary Building

Choose a word from the list that fits each clue. The first one is done for you. Cross off the words as you work.

~~benches~~	miles per hour	prevent	station
force	passengers	race	straighter
governor	platform	service	tracks

1. You can sit on them. _____benches_____

2. This person is the leader of a U.S. state. _____

3. This means *go fast*. _____

4. This is how fast something goes. _____

5. You wait **on** this for a train. _____

6. You wait **in** this for a train. _____

7. This means *less curved*. _____

8. These will ride on the *Acela*. _____

9. Trains run on these. _____

10. Another word for *power*. _____

11. It means *stop something from happening*. _____

12. You get this at a restaurant. Sometimes it's good, and sometimes it's bad. _____

> **Japan's railroad system carries over 20 million passengers every day. It is the busiest in the world.**

ACADEMIC POWER STRATEGY

Study in a group to better understand information from your classes. Study groups can be very helpful. Sometimes, you may be confused when you study alone. Or, you might have questions that you can't answer by yourself. When you study with a group of people, you can:

- learn from each other
- ask questions
- get answers
- enjoy yourself

(continued on next page)

Working in a study group will help you do better in your classes. You might also make friends who will help you in future classes at school.

Apply the Strategy

Form a study group. Follow these steps:

1. Write down the names, phone numbers, and e-mail addresses of everyone in the group on a piece of paper. Write clearly.

2. Make a copy of the list for each person in the group.

3. Compare your schedules. Find a time to study for one hour each week.

4. Decide on a place to study.

5. Write your study group time on your calendar.

After you meet your study group, write in your journal about it. Answer these questions:

- Was it helpful? How?

- How can it be better next time?

- What did you learn?

◆ **Getting Ready to Read**

Do you have a car? Why or why not? Work in groups to talk about these questions. Write your ideas on the chart. Then share your ideas with the rest of your class.

Advantages (good things) about having a car	Disadvantages (bad things) about having a car

Vocabulary Check

Look at the words and phrases below. Put a check mark next to the ones that you know. Talk with your class about the words and phrases you don't know. Write the new words you learn in your Vocabulary Log.

_____ battery   _____ financial   _____ start from scratch

_____ commuting   _____ founder   _____ take seriously

_____ decades   _____ frustrations   _____ unit

_____ designed   _____ popular   _____ vehicles

_____ emission   _____ profit

_____ engineers   _____ recharged

 Read

Reading 3: Electric Cars

1   For many **decades,** people have dreamed of electric cars. However, making them has been more difficult than anyone predicted. But the dream of an electric car may finally be coming true.

2   People were interested in making electric cars as early as the 1840s. One small electric car was made then, but it didn't work well. Then, in 1912, General Motors' **founder** Billy Durant produced an electric truck. However, these electric **vehicles** were not made for the public to buy.

3   By the early 1990s, because of growing air pollution, the California Air Resources Board (CARB) made a new rule. The Board said that by 1998, the seven major automakers—GM, Ford, Chrysler, Honda, Toyota, Nissan, and Mazda—would have to make 2 percent of their cars and trucks **emission**-free. That number will rise to 5 percent in 2001 and 10 percent by 2003. Therefore, automakers had to begin to **take** electric cars **seriously.**

4   General Motors was the first to try again. The challenge was difficult. An electric car needs a **battery.** But batteries are heavy and don't work well. None of them could power a car far enough or long enough. The **engineers** had to **start from scratch.** There were many **frustrations.**

5   The **financial** challenges were also great. The new technology cost a lot. It seemed that the car would be so expensive that no one would buy it. General Motors didn't think it could make a **profit** on the electric cars.

Henry Ford invented the Model T car in 1908.

6   At last, they succeeded. The car they built was called the EV1. It became available in California and Arizona in 1998. It is the first electric car **designed** and sold by a large automobile company.

7   The EV1 runs on a heavy, T-shaped battery. The battery is about 18 inches long and $4\frac{1}{2}$ inches wide. Because the car doesn't use gasoline, it does not pollute the air.

8   After about 70 miles of driving, the car's battery must be **recharged** by connecting it to a special recharging **unit.** Recharging takes three hours.

9   Because of the battery, many people think that electric cars are not convenient. It is not possible to drive them long distances without taking a long break to recharge. Others think that they are perfect for **commuting,** and short trips.

10   Automakers hope they can improve electric cars. With the changing laws and concern about pollution, they are sure these cars will be **popular.**

◀ **After You Read**

1. When was the first electric car made?

2. Why are people interested in electric cars today?

3. What is CARB?

4. What is the EV1?

5. Who makes the EV1?

6. How far will the car go on one charging of the battery?

7. What does it use for power?

8. How long does it take to recharge the battery?

9. What are the advantages of the EV1?

10. What are the disadvantages?

11. Would you like to have an electric car?

12. Do you think electric cars will become popular?

◇ Vocabulary Building

Draw a line from the word or phrase in Column A to its correct meaning in Column B.

A	B
1. a storage cell	A. popular
2. a gain	B. to recharge
3. well-liked	C. a decade
4. to give energy again	D. financial
5. gases	E. vehicle
6. a person who starts a company or organization	F. a profit
7. relating to money	G. a design
8. a plan	H. a battery
9. ten years	I. to commute
10. form of transportation	J. emissions
11. to travel back and forth	K. a founder

LANGUAGE LEARNING STRATEGY

Use a graphic organizer to help you organize information. A graphic organizer can be a picture or a diagram. It can contain the topic, the main ideas, and the examples from a reading. For example, a graphic organizer for "Free Bike Programs" might look like this:

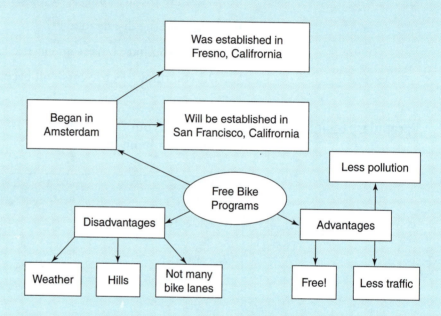

Apply the Strategy

Now complete a graphic organizer for "Electric Cars."

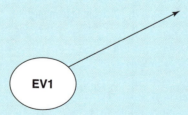

© CNN

TUNING IN: "Subway Etiquette"

The title of this video is "Subway Etiquette." What does the word "etiquette" mean? Discuss this word with your class. Give some examples of etiquette.

You will hear the following words and phrases in the video. Put a check mark next to the words and phrases that you know. Talk with your class about the ones you don't know. Write the new words you learn in your Vocabulary Log.

_____ graffiti   _____ politeness

_____ manners   _____ rugby scrimmage

_____ optimist   _____ shove

_____ panhandling

In the video, you will hear numbers which tell how many subway lines, subway stations, miles of track, and passengers there are on the New York subway system. While you watch the video, listen for the numbers and write them in the blanks below.

_____ lines

_____ stations

_____ miles of track

_____ passengers per year

Discuss the following questions with your class.

1. Why did New York City start politeness training?

2. What do the subway workers do?

3. Why did the city paint orange boxes in the subway stations?

4. Do the subway workers think the politeness training will work?

◆ **Getting Ready to Read**

Before you read "The Wrights Were Right," think about what you already know about airplanes and flying. Answer these questions with a group of students. Write your answers on the board or on a piece of paper.

1. What do you know about airplanes? Write down everything you know about airplanes.

2. Do you know about the history of airplanes? Write down everything you know about the history of airplanes.

Vocabulary Check

Look at the words below. Put a check mark next to the ones that you know. Talk with your class about the words you don't know. Write the new ones in your Vocabulary Log.

_____ ability	_____ flight	_____ lightweight
_____ century	_____ gliders	_____ owe
_____ conducted	_____ intrigued	_____ propeller
_____ descend	_____ inventions	_____ publishing
_____ experiments	_____ kites	_____ self-propelled

Read

Reading 4: The Wrights Were Right

1   At the beginning of the 20th **century,** many people thought that it was impossible for humans to fly. Orville and Wilbur Wright, however, were two brothers who thought differently. In fact, we **owe** our **ability** to travel by airplane to the **inventions** of the Wright brothers. In 1903, the Wright brothers invented the first successful **self-propelled** airplane.

2   Wilbur Wright, the older brother, was born on April 16, 1867, in Millville, Indiana. Orville Wright was the younger of the two brothers. He was born on August 19, 1871, in Dayton, Ohio. These two brothers often worked together. In the 1880s, their first project was **publishing** a newspaper. Later, in the 1890s, they became interested in bicycles. They started the "Wright Cycle Company." This company was located in Dayton, Ohio, and it built and sold bicycles.

3   In 1896, Orville and Wilbur heard about the **experiments** of European inventors who were experimenting with **flight.** Orville and Wilbur became **intrigued** by this idea, and they started their own experiments. First they worked with **kites.** They **conducted** tests to see how the kites could stay in the air. After they worked with kites, they decided to do experiments with **gliders.** In the experiments with gliders, the Wright brothers tested many things. They practiced making the glider rise in the air. They also practiced turning the glider and making the glider **descend.** They made more than 700 glider flights in their experiments.

4   But the Wright brothers were not satisfied. They wanted to make an airplane that had an engine to give it power. They needed to find a powerful engine, but the powerful engines were too heavy. The heavy engines prevented the airplane from flying. The Wright brothers asked several car makers to help them design a **lightweight,** powerful engine. None of the car makers wanted to help them, so Orville and Wilbur worked with another inventor named Charles Taylor to make their own engine. They designed a 12-to-16 horsepower[1] engine as well as a **propeller** for their airplane.

5   On December 17, 1903, the Wright brothers went to Kitty Hawk, North Carolina, to test their airplane. On this day, Orville successfully flew the airplane. It was the first time anyone had ever flown in a self-propelled airplane. Later, in 1909, the Wright brothers built an airplane that could carry two people and could fly as fast as 125 miles per hour. Because of the Wright brothers' hard work, we now can fly anyplace in the world. Their experiments and inventions have made our lives both more exciting and more convenient.

 **After You Read**

1. What did the Wright brothers invent?

2. Where were the brothers born?

3. What kinds of businesses did they have?

4. What did they experiment with before they made the airplane?

5. What problems did they have with the engine?

6. Where did they fly an airplane for the first time?

7. Who flew the airplane the first time?

[1]"Horsepower" refers to the amount of power an engine has. It is an old measurement that estimates the number of horses it would take to do the same job as the engine.

LANGUAGE LEARNING STRATEGY

Make a time line to help you understand events in your reading. You will often see dates or times in your reading. Sometimes, there are many dates to keep track of. Sometimes, also, they are not presented in order. You can make a time line to help you organize the dates. This will help you understand your reading better.

Apply the Strategy

Read "The Wrights Were Right" again and find the dates and events there. Fill in the information on the timeline. The events go on the top, and the dates go on the bottom of the line.

Wilbur born

1867

PUTTING IT ALL TOGETHER

Before you read, discuss this list of words and phrases with your class.

——— advanced technology   ——— on course

——— combat aircraft   ——— ordinary

——— fuel   ——— plastic composites

——— metal alloys   ——— soar

——— navigation systems   ——— sophisticated

——— obstacles

Find these words and phrases in the reading and highlight them. For ones that you don't know, look at the context in the reading. Then, if you still don't know the words, look them up in your dictionary, and explain them to a partner.

Aircraft

Less than 100 years ago, even the fastest ship took more than a week to cross the Atlantic Ocean. Today, most jet airliners (large passenger planes) can make this 3,000-mile (4,800-km) journey in less than seven hours. Aircraft are the fastest way to travel because they can soar straight over obstacles such as mountains and oceans. Powerful jet engines enable the fastest combat aircraft to reach speeds of 2,000 miles per hour (mph) (3,200 km/h)—three times faster than sound. Even ordinary jet airliners fly at more than 530 mph (850km/h). Modern aircraft are packed with advanced technology to help them fly safely and economically at great speed. Sophisticated electronic control and navigation systems keep the airplane on course. Computer-designed wings help cut fuel costs. And airframes (aircraft bodies) are made of metal alloys and plastic composites that are lightweight and strong.

1. Reread the paragraph and make a graphic organizer about airplanes. Compare your graphic organizer with your classmates.

2. Create five flash cards that ask questions about airplanes.

CHECK YOUR PROGRESS

On a scale of 1 to 5, rate how well you've mastered the goals set at the beginning of the chapter:

1 2 3 4 5   use a graphic organizer.

1 2 3 4 5   study in a group.

1 2 3 4 5   use quotations.

1 2 3 4 5   make a time line.

1 2 3 4 5   use flash cards to study for tests.

If you've given yourself a 3 or lower on any of these goals:

- visit the *Tapestry* web site for additional practice.
- ask your instructor for extra help.
- review the sections of the chapter that you found difficult.
- work with a partner or study group to further your progress.

L ook at the photo. Talk with your class about these questions:

- Do you enjoy fast food?
- What is your favorite kind of fast food?
- Why do people eat fast food?

A WORLD OF FAST FOOD

Everyone has to eat to live. However, more and more, eating *fast* has become a way of life. People in the United States have eaten fast food for many years. This habit is moving to other countries as well. Of course, fast food in different countries is not always just hamburgers and pizza. Although American-style fast food is popular, local types of fast food are, too. This chapter looks at the world of fast food.

Setting Goals

In this chapter you will learn how to:

◈ read tables and graphs.

◈ read more quickly.

◈ improve your performance on essay tests.

◈ avoid distractions when you study.

◈ use ordering words.

Which goal is most important to you? _____

_____

Why? _____

Talk about your answers with your class.

◆ Getting Started

Who likes fast food? Find three classmates that eat fast food. Ask these three questions. Put the information in the chart.

	Student 1	Student 2	Student 3
1. How often do you eat fast food?			
2. What is your favorite restaurant?			
3. Do you eat too much fast food?			

Compare and talk about your answers with your class.

◆ Getting Ready to Read

The first reading tells about a country that loves fast food. Talk about these questions with your class before you begin:

1. What's an invasion?

2. Do you think there are too many fast food restaurants where you live?

3. Does your city need more fast food restaurants? Why or why not?

4. Can food be fast *and* good? Explain your answer.

> **There are more than 24,500 McDonald's restaurants in 116 countries.**

Vocabulary Check

Look at the words and phrases below. Put a check mark next to the ones that you know. Talk with your class about the words and phrases you don't know. Write the new words you learn in your Vocabulary Log.

_____ advertise	_____ consumers	_____ invaded
_____ capital city	_____ convenient	_____ pork
_____ chain restaurants	_____ craze	_____ treats
_____ compete	_____ creative	

Read

Reading 1: Fast Food Invasion

1 American fast food restaurants have **invaded** the island of Jamaica. It's a peaceful invasion, but local restaurant owners don't think it's a friendly one. Kentucky Fried Chicken (KFC), Burger King, Pizza Hut, and TCBY (The Country's Best Yogurt) have all opened restaurants around Jamaica. There is no sign this **craze** will slow down. Fast food restaurant owners don't want to say how well their businesses are doing. They will say hungry **consumers** are spending millions of dollars.

2 Recently, Subway, a popular American sandwich shop, opened a fifth restaurant in Kingston, the **capital city** of Jamaica. McDonald's has three restaurants there, as well.

3 Jamaicans have always liked fast food. The patty, a local meat-filled pie, has been a favorite for decades. Other spicy local **treats** like jerked chicken and jerked **pork** are still very popular.

4 However, the popularity of Burger King and Pizza Hut have influenced business. Smaller restaurants that sell local dishes have to try hard to stay in business. They don't have the money to **advertise** like the big American **chain restaurants** do.

5 One of those local stores is Tastee's, makers of the patty. Tastee's has been in business for 25 years. But now, it is trying to keep its popularity. Because the patty is cheaper than American fast food, it still sells well at Tastee's.

However, Tastee's has had to add different kinds of food to their menu to **compete** with American restaurants.

6 "The patty is not as expensive as the pizza or the burger. So, we still sell a lot of them," says a manager at Tastee's. A patty is smaller than a hamburger, but very filling. It sells for 46 cents. A hamburger costs $2.46 and a pizza costs from between $5.80 and $15.

7 Jamaicans have difficult work schedules. This is the main reason for their interest in fast food. "It's very **convenient**," says one diner. "People are busy and don't have time to make a meal at home. They eat fast food when they're going to work and coming home from work."

8 The result is that Jamaicans are not eating healthy food. Fast food is cheaper than healthy food. Healthy food takes more time to shop for and prepare. Of course, Jamaicans would like to eat food that is both healthy and fast. To help with this problem, the yogurt shop TCBY has been **creative.** They have four stores in Jamaica that sell yogurt as well as low-fat ice cream.

9 Many fast food restaurants are starting to offer more healthy foods. It seems that the fast food restaurants will do anything to keep their customers happy. Their success will probably last a long time in Jamaica, and in other parts of the world.

After You Read

1. What new restaurants have opened in Jamaica?

2. How much money do Jamaicans spend on fast food?

3. What is a patty?

4. Why are small local restaurants having trouble?

5. How is Tastee's trying to compete with American fast food restaurants?

6. Why is fast food popular in Jamaica?

7. What kind of food does TCBY sell?

8. Why will fast food restaurants stay popular in Jamaica?

9. If you went to Jamaica, would you eat Jamaican food or American-style fast food? Why?

◆Vocabulary Building

The words in bold are from the Vocabulary Check. Fill in the information you are asked for relating to these words. Work with a partner.

1. Name three **capital cities:** _____, _____, and _____

2. Name three **chain restaurants:** _____, _____, and _____

3. Name three kinds of **treats:** _____, _____, and _____

4. Name three modern **crazes:** _____, _____, and _____

5. Name three things that make life more **convenient:** _____, _____, and _____

ACADEMIC POWER STRATEGY

Avoid distractions when you study. Distractions are things that keep you from doing your work. For example, a telephone call, the television, or a noisy neighbor might be a distraction. When you are studying, you should stay away from distractions. One place that is filled with distractions is the school cafeteria, especially during lunch time. If you plan to study in the cafeteria, you may be distracted by being hungry, by eating, or by friends that you might see there. Also, avoid studying in front of the television. Instead, choose a quiet place and pick a time when you feel your best. By avoiding distractions when you are studying, you will get more work done in less time. This will leave you more time to do the things you enjoy.

Apply the Strategy

Answer these questions to try to identify and avoid distractions when you study:

1. Where do you study most of the time? _____

   _____

2. What distractions are there in that place? _____

   _____

3. How can you avoid those distractions? _____

   _____

   _____

4. When do you usually study? _____

   _____

5. Are there distractions at that time of day? _____

   _____

6. How can you avoid those distractions? _____

   _____

   _____

Discuss your answers with a partner. Give each other advice on avoiding distractions.

TUNING IN: "Fast Food"

In the video, you will hear these phrases, which are related to being in a rush. Discuss these phrases with your class. Write the new phrases you learn in your Vocabulary Log.

© CNN

_____ beat the clock   _____ fast track

_____ fast lane   _____ rush hour

Before you watch the video, talk about these questions with your classmates.

1. How much time do you spend each day preparing your meals?

2. Do you buy fast food meals for yourself and your family? Why or why not?

Now watch the video and complete the following charts:

Money Spent on Eating Out		
year _____ % _____		
year _____ % _____		
year _____ % _____		

Why We Dine Out		
% _____ reason _____		
% _____ reason _____		
% _____ reason _____		

Food Experts in the Video	
name	job
1. _____	_____
2. _____	_____

Watch the video again and talk about these questions with your class:

1. Who is June Cleaver?

2. Why is she mentioned in this video?

3. What's missing in today's kitchen, according to this video? Why?

4. Do the cookbooks in the video look interesting or helpful? Why or why not?

> **Tell me what you eat: I will tell you what you are.**
>
> **—BRILLAT-SAVARIN**

LANGUAGE LEARNING STRATEGY

Learn to read tables and graphs to increase your understanding of what you read. Most people think learning to read well means learning to read essays, stories, or books. However, there are many different kinds of reading. Learning to read tables and graphs will help you in your studies. Tables and graphs often contain information that is useful and important to the reader. Sometimes, this information makes an essay clearer.

Apply the Strategy

This table gives information about some fast food. As you read the table, think about these facts:

- An average person needs 2,000 calories a day from his or her food.
- Only 30% of those calories should be from fat. This is equal to about 65 grams of fat.

Burger King	Calories	% of Calories from fat	Grams of fat
CROISSAN'WICH® with Sausage, Egg & Cheese	530	70	41
Hash Brown Rounds—Small	240	58	15
WHOPPER® Sandwich	660	55	40
DOUBLE WHOPPER® With Cheese Sandwich	1010	59	67
Small French Fries	250	48	13
Chocolate Shake—Small	330	18	7
McDonald's	**Calories**	**% of Calories from fat**	**Grams of fat**
Hamburger	260	31	9
Big Mac®	560	50	31
Fish Filet Deluxe™	560	45	28
Super Size® French Fries	540	43	26
Garden Salad	35	0	0
Egg McMuffin®	290	38	12
Pizza Hut (1 slice of a medium pizza)			
Cheese	309	25	9
Pepperoni	301	25	8
Italian Sausage	363	35	14
Veggie Lover's	281	20	6
TCBY			
Nonfat frozen yogurt	110	0	0
No sugar added nonfat frozen yogurt	80	0	0
No sugar low-fat ice cream	100	25	2.5

1. Plan your breakfast, lunch, and dinner from this list. Eat only about 2,000 calories and 30% fat (65 grams). What will you eat?

   Breakfast: _____

   _____

   Lunch: _____

   _____

   Dinner: _____

   _____

   Would you enjoy eating these meals?

2. Which two items have the most grams of fat? _____

   and _____

3. Which restaurant offers the healthiest food? _____

4. Which restaurant offers the least healthy food? _____

5. Is fish a better choice than a hamburger at McDonald's? Why or why not? _____

6. Is it possible to eat healthy food from these menus? _____

   What are the best choices? _____

   _____

◆**Getting Ready to Read**

The next reading tells the story of the first McDonald's restaurant. Before you read, talk with your class about these questions:

1. What's a *landmark?*

2. Is a McDonald's restaurant part of history?

3. Do you think the first McDonald's restaurant should be a landmark?

Vocabulary Check

Look at the words and phrases below. Put a check mark next to the ones that you know. Talk with your class about the words and phrases you don't know. Write the new words you learn in your Vocabulary Log.

Hamburgers were not commonly made in America until the early 20th century. The first hamburger fast food chain was White Castle, founded in 1916 by J. Walter Anderson of Wichita, Kansas. He sold five cent hamburgers along with french fries and colas.

_____ abandoned

_____ arches

_____ boards

_____ corporation

_____ cultural

_____ dates

_____ denies

_____ drive-thru window

_____ earthquake

_____ excuse

_____ historians

_____ invent

_____ landmark

_____ register

_____ repaired

_____ resident

_____ symbol

◆**Read**

Reading 2: Old McDonald's

1 The first McDonald's only sold hamburgers and french fries, but it became a **cultural symbol.** Now, citizens in the Southern California city of Downey are trying to save the small building—the first McDonald's. **Historians** say it is a **landmark** that is part of American culture. McDonald's says the building should be torn down.

2   Some people laugh at McDonald's being a cultural landmark. But the restaurant in Downey, California, is the oldest **Golden Arches**[1] in America. It was built in 1953, and has the earliest McDonald's building design.

3   Some teenagers came here on their first **dates.** Others came here after high school football games. Some got their first jobs here. Many people have good memories of this old McDonald's. They're angry that the building is in danger, and that their memories are as well.

4   McDonald's explains the building was damaged in an **earthquake** and had to be

[1]The Golden Arches is the symbol of McDonald's restaurants. You can see them in the photo on page 108.

torn down. Many people in the town of Downey don't believe that reason, though.

5 Martina Pavel says, "I think it's terrible. They are using the earthquake as an **excuse.** It's a big lie."

6 Another Downey **resident** says, "I am so upset. They don't respect the public at all. They haven't even tried. They could make some small changes and make it a good restaurant again.

7 The McDonald's **Corporation** says it was losing money there. There was no room for a **drive-thru window,** or for indoor seating. After the earthquake, they say it wasn't possible to fix it. They want to build a copy of this building at another location instead.

8 Building inspectors say the building can be **repaired,** but it will be expensive—$300,000. Many people say that McDonald's can certainly pay that amount. Some think that McDonald's real reason for wanting to close down the restaurant is not the money.

9 Modern McDonald's restaurants often have a sign that says a man named Ray Kroc opened his first McDonald's restaurant in Illinois in 1955. But Mr. Kroc learned the fast food business from Dick and Mac McDonald in Downey. Later Mr. Kroc bought their restaurants. Many people in Downey think McDonald's is trying to change history. McDonald's Corporation **denies** it's trying to remove the McDonald brothers from history.

10 However, this explanation makes sense to the historians. One historian said, "We should not rewrite the past. Ray Kroc did not **invent** McDonald's. The McDonald brothers did."

11 Now, a group of historians wants the building to be put on the National **Register** of Historic Places so that the city of Downey will be able to stop McDonald's from tearing the building down. McDonald's is angry, and has **abandoned** the building.

12 Everyone hopes the McDonald's Corporation and the city of Downey will find peace. The building is still there, but **boards** cover the windows. Even so, people drive by to remember their McDonald's. They take pictures of a moment in history before it's taken away.

After You Read

1. What did the first McDonald's sell?

2. When and where was the first McDonald's built?

3. Why do some people want to save the first McDonald's?

4. Why does McDonald's Corporation say it shut the restaurant down?

5. Why don't some citizens of Downey believe this?

6. Where did the name *McDonald's* come from?

7. Who is Ray Kroc?

8. Whose story do you believe, McDonald's' or the historians'?

9. What is the building like now?

10. Do you think the building should be saved? Why or why not?

McDonald's opened its 25,000th restaurant in June, 1999.

Vocabulary Building

Write the correct word in the blanks. Cross the words off as you work.

abandoned	denies	invent	repaired
boards	earthquake	landmark	residents

cultural   excuse   register   symbol

dates   historians

1. When a building is badly damaged in a/an _____,

   it should be _____.

2. A group of _____ think the first

   McDonald's is a _____.

3. They want it put on the National Historic _____.

4. Many _____ of Downey think McDonald's

   is giving them a/an _____.

5. McDonald's _____ that they are trying to rewrite

   history.

6. Ray Kroc did not _____ McDonald's.

7. Many people think the old McDonald's is a _____

   _____.

8. Many teenagers had their first _____ at McDonald's.

9. McDonald's has _____ the old building.

10. There are _____ on the windows.

◆Getting Ready to Read

LANGUAGE LEARNING STRATEGY

Read more quickly to increase your understanding of a reading. Many people believe they have to read more slowly in order to understand better. In fact, for many people, reading slowly is the problem. When they read slowly, they read word by word. When they read like this, they sometimes don't understand the meanings of phrases and sentences—in other words, they don't see how the words work together.

From time to time, it is a good idea to think about your reading speed. You can test your speed by writing down the time it takes to read something and then counting the words. If you keep a record

(continued on next page)

of your time, you can test yourself and see if you've improved. A good goal is 100 words a minute. How fast are you reading?

Apply the Strategy

Read "Food from Your Computer" as quickly as you can, while still understanding the ideas. In the space provided, write down your time, and see how many words you are reading each minute. Later in the book, you can check to see if you have improved your reading speed.

Vocabulary Check

Look at the words below. Put a check mark next to the words that you know. Talk with your class about the words you don't know. Write the new words you learn in your Vocabulary Log.

_____ accounts	_____ equipment
_____ charging	_____ Internet
_____ computers	_____ on hold
_____ confirms	_____ online
_____ convince	_____ order (noun)
_____ delivery	_____ takeout
_____ e-mails (verb)	

◆ **Read**

Reading 3: Food from Your Computer

Starting time _____:_____

1 Food.com[1] is a new company that lets customers order lunch and dinner from their **computers.** About 12,000 restaurants in the United States have signed up to be part of the service. The company has put restaurants' menus **online.** Now, people with **Internet accounts** can place an order for **takeout** or **delivery.**

2 Customers are spending more money on takeout and delivery from restaurants than ever before. Food.com hopes to **convince** people that ordering from their computers is quick and convenient. They think it is a better way to order food than using the telephone.

3 Consumers go to Food.com on their computers, then type in their street address and phone number. The computer shows them which restaurants have takeout and delivery service in their neighborhood. It also shows them the menus, so they can decide what they want to eat.

[1]Read this as "food dot com."

4   Next, a customer **e-mails** an **order** to Food.com. The company's computers change the e-mail message into a telephone message. Then they send the order by telephone to the restaurant. A restaurant worker **confirms** that they received it. They return a message that says how long it'll take to deliver the food.

5   Food.com also sends an e-mail message to the customer. It tells them when the food will arrive. The whole ordering process takes about seven minutes. Finally, the restaurant or a delivery service brings the food.

6   But some people say it's not easier than using the phone. Jeanne LeBlanc says, "I don't understand the new system. It's not easier than calling the restaurant. And I like to eat lunch out, anyway."

7   John Price likes the new system, though. "I can look at the menu, make my choice, and send it in just a couple of minutes. Sometimes if I call, they put me **on hold.** Or, I don't have their menu, so they have to read it to me. It takes a long time. Besides, I don't like talking on the telephone very much. So, I'm very happy with the idea."

8   Food.com makes money by **charging** a restaurant $400 to put its menu online. Then they charge $50 a month to keep the menu on the Food.com website. The company also takes 5 percent of every order placed through the computer. Restaurants don't have to buy any special **equipment.** They just need a telephone.

9   Lots of Americans like to have their food delivered, so this idea might become very successful. Takeout and delivery sales reached $126 billion in 1997. Research shows that it will reach $195 billion by 2007. Customers spend 30 percent more when they order on their computers than when they go to a restaurant to eat. Food.com may become a very popular spot to eat.

Ending time: _____:_____

Total time: _____ mins.

Divide 443 by your time = _____ words per minute

How close were you to 100 words per minute?

◆ **After You Read**

1. What is Food.com?

2. How many restaurants have signed up with the service?

3. Who can use Food.com?

4. How does the Food.com system work?

5. How long does it take to place an order?

6. Do you think it's easier than using a telephone? Why or why not?

7. Why do some customers like the system?

8. How does Food.com make money?

9. What do restaurants need to be part of Food.com?

10. Why might this way of ordering food become very successful?

11. How often do you order dinner for takeout or delivery? Why?

Grammar You Can Use

Ordering Words

"Food from Your Computer" tells you about a *process* of ordering food from the Internet. It uses words such as *first, second, third, next, then, finally,* and so forth to show the order in which you do things. These words are commonly used to show steps.

Here are some steps for ordering from Food.com. Put them in order, then write complete sentences telling what to do. Use ordering words.

Choose a restaurant.

Choose the food.

Eat the food.

Go to the Food.com web site.

Read the menu.

Send an e-mail message with your order.

Type in your name and address.

Wait for an e-mail message to tell you when the food is coming.

_____

_____

_____

_____

_____

_____

_____

Vocabulary Building

Put these words into one of the two following categories. Some words might belong in more than one category.

accounts	consumer	equipment	order
charge	delivery	Internet	takeout
confirm	e-mail	online	

Words related to computers	Words related to restaurants

Test-Taking Tip

Improve your performance on essay tests. Essay tests worry students more than almost any kind of test. Here are some tips for preparing for essay tests:

- Review your notes well.
- Try to predict the essay questions.
- Practice writing short answers to your questions.
- Understand the task. Ask your teacher if you can use books or notes. Ask if there will be one question, or if you will have to answer several shorter ones.
- Plan your time during the test. Take time to think about your answer before you write, and leave time to check your work.
- At the test, ask your teacher if you don't understand the essay question.

If you plan well, you will be confident about taking essay exams.

◆**Getting Ready to Read**   The last reading in this chapter talks about fast food on the Island of Singapore. It shows that fast food doesn't have to be hamburgers and pizza. Before you read, write about these questions in your journal:

1. What is your favorite food?

2. What kind of restaurant do you like to visit?

3. Is there a food from another culture that you enjoy? (Don't include American food.) Describe that food.

Vocabulary Check

Look at the words below. Put a check mark next to the words that you know. Talk with your class about the words you don't know. Write the new words you learn in your Vocabulary Log.

_____ bazaar	_____ neat	_____ temple
_____ cashiers	_____ playground	_____ token
_____ chutneys	_____ skyscrapers	_____ vegetarian
_____ curries		

◆Read

Reading 4: Fast Food with a Difference

1 On Serangoon Road in Singapore, something interesting is happening: fast food with a difference. This street is surrounded by **skyscrapers,** modern shopping malls, and office buildings. It looks like a South Indian **bazaar.** It has Indian shops. In Thosai[1] cafés, food is served on banana leaves. And it also has an Indian **vegetarian** fast food restaurant called Komala's. This restaurant is becoming as popular as McDonald's.

2 Komala's looks like an American fast food restaurant. It has plastic chairs and tables that are attached to the floor. There is also a children's **playground** in the restaurant. What makes it different is its menu, which is all Indian and vegetarian.

3 It offers more choices of food than most fast food restaurants do. The menu is on the wall above the **cashiers.** The prices are cheap, and once the orders are taken and paid for, the customer is given a **token** to present to the food counter. The customer turns in the token and picks up the food.

4 The food is ready in about two minutes. If it's for takeout, it is wrapped and put in a bag. If the customer eats in the restaurant, they eat from metal plates and cups, on a tray covered with paper. This paper shows pictures of the food that is available at Komala's.

5 The menu offers more than ten kinds of thosai, steamed buns, and many other types of Indian foods. These come accompanied by **curries** and **chutneys.** There are also mini-meals for children, which include lassi, a sweetened yogurt drink, and ice cream.

6 On Sundays, a lot of Indian families come here for a vegetarian dinner after going to the nearby **temple.** Komala's is air-conditioned, the seats are good, the service is very fast, and it's very **neat** and clean. This isn't true of other restaurants in the neighborhood.

7 "This is an amazing place," says Sim Tang, a Chinese office worker who eats at Komala's after work. "My Indian friends told me about it. I have come here ever since. I enjoy some thosai and tea."

8 Komala's is so popular, it may open in India, Australia, and Malaysia. More will open in Singapore soon. The restaurant owner says that when people eat at Komala's, they feel like part of the international community.

[1]Thosai is a type of South Indian pancake.

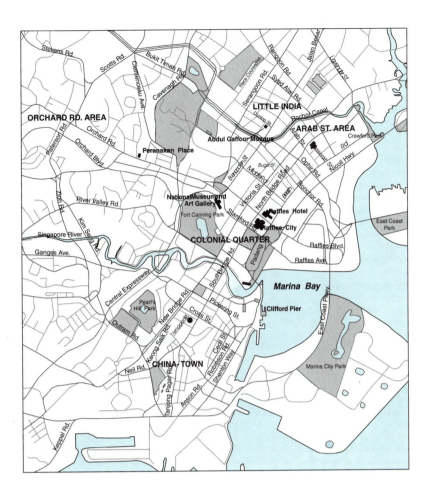

After You Read

1. What is Komala's?

2. Where is Komala's?

3. What is the neighborhood it is in like?

4. What does Komala's look like?

5. What kinds of food can you buy there?

6. Why is Komala's compared to American fast food restaurants?

7. How is it different from American fast food restaurants?

8. What is Komala's future likely to be?

9. What did the restaurant owner mean when he said, "When people eat at Komala's, they feel like a part of the international community"?

10. Do you think you would enjoy the food at Komala's? Why or why not?

◆ **Vocabulary Building**

Match the word in Column A to its meaning in Column B. Draw a line to the correct answer.

A	B
A. chutney	1. a marketplace
B. a skyscraper	2. relish of fruit and/or spices
C. a token	3. a spicy Indian dish
D. a temple	4. a place where children have fun
E. clean	5. a very tall building
F. a playground	6. a house of worship
G. vegetarian	7. a coin
H. curry	8. neat
I. a bazaar	9. no meat

PUTTING IT ALL TOGETHER

This crossword puzzle uses some words from your readings.

Across

4. Cooked potatoes you eat with hamburgers
6. Short for *advertisement*
7. A popular drink in Asia
8. People who eat at restaurants
10. Food from a restaurant you bring home
11. Lettuce, tomatoes, and dressing

Down

1. You place an _____ at a restaurant for your food.
2. McDonald's Golden _____
3. Food a restaurant brings to your house
4. A Whopper hamburger has many grams of this.
5. Meat in a bun
9. Clean

CHECK YOUR PROGRESS

On a scale of 1 to 5, rate how well you've mastered the goals set at the beginning of the chapter:

1 2 3 4 5   read tables and graphs.

1 2 3 4 5   read more quickly.

1 2 3 4 5   improve your performance on essay tests.

1 2 3 4 5   avoid distractions when you study.

1 2 3 4 5   use ordering words.

If you've given yourself a 3 or lower on any of these goals:

- visit the *Tapestry* web site for additional practice.
- ask your instructor for extra help.
- review the sections of the chapter that you found difficult.
- work with a partner or study group to further your progress.

L ook at the photos. Talk with your class about these
questions:

- What is happening in these photos?
- How are the photos different from each other?
- Have you ever attended a wedding? What was it like?
- What are weddings like in your native culture?

LOVE AND MARRIAGE

Weddings are important in nearly every culture. And every culture has its own wedding traditions. This chapter looks at some customs from different cultures. It also looks at the history of some wedding customs.

Setting Goals

In this chapter, you will learn how to:

- identify arguments in your reading.

- identify the main idea in your reading.

- organize your study area.

- use old tests to help study for new ones.

- understand adverbs and adjectives.

Which goal is most important to you? _____

_____

Why? _____

Talk about your answers with your class.

◆ **Getting Started**

Write in your journal about *weddings*. You can write anything you want, or you can use these questions to help you begin:

1. Why are weddings important to families?

2. What is a tradition?

3. What are some important wedding traditions?

4. Describe an important wedding in your life (your own, a brother's, a friend's, and so forth).

◆ **Getting Ready to Read**

Talk about what you wrote in your journal with your class. Express your opinion about traditions, and explain important wedding traditions in your native culture.

> **Marriage is a weaving together of families, of two souls with their individual fates and destinies, of time and eternity–everyday life married to the timeless mysteries of the soul.**
>
> **—THOMAS MOORE**

Vocabulary Check

Look at the words below. Put a check mark next to the words that you know. Talk with your class about the words you don't know. Write the new words you learn in your Vocabulary Log.

_____ abuse (verb)	_____ commercialized	_____ groom
_____ asset	_____ custom	_____ individual
_____ bride	_____ debated	_____ pride
_____ burden	_____ equal	_____ rights
_____ cattle	_____ generosity	_____ support
_____ chores	_____ get rid of	

◆ **Read**

Reading 1: Brides for Sale?

1 *Lobola* is the African **custom** of paying for a **bride.** Although it is an old custom, not everyone in African cultures is happy with it. In fact, it is being **debated** in Botswana.

2   Many people, including many women, **support** payment of lobola. They explain that in Tswana culture, a marriage means joining a family, not just marrying an **individual.** The idea of marrying into a family is very African. A woman does not get married to just the man. Through marriage, the young woman's family loses their daughter as she then becomes a part of her husband's family. Lobola is a way to show thanks. It is a form of **generosity** in African culture.

3   In its traditional form, they also explain, the groom's family gave **cattle** to the bride's family. But, it didn't matter whether the

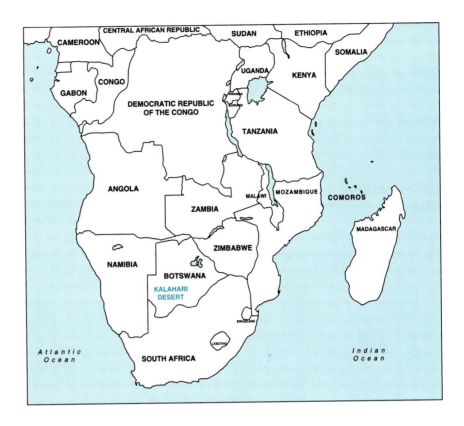

family owned cattle or not. A man only had to pay what he could afford—if he had no cattle, he could give something else, even the smallest form of payment. The tradition of lobola was a matter of **pride.**

4   Today, lobola is often given in cash. But its supporters say it is not about the purchase of a bride. Lobola is meant to join two families together. They know that some people **abuse** the custom. But, they believe that the tradition should not be tossed out because it has many positive effects. Rather than **get rid of** it, many believe it should just be explained better.

5   However, many others say this custom should be stopped. They think it has become **commercialized.** Families make lots of demands on the **groom.** They think this makes lobola look very bad.

6   They argue that in Africa's past, a girl was an **asset** at home. She did the cooking and other household **chores.** When a family lost that child through marriage, it demanded payment. Today, they think that lobola has changed into a useless tradition. In this custom, a man is buying the right to control a woman. They say women are individuals with **rights.** In today's world, parents do not have to be paid for a bride, because their male and female children are **equal.** They all work and make contributions to the household.

7   They believe that paying lobola makes it seem like a man is buying a pair of shoes or a bicycle, instead of getting married. They also argue that it is often a financial **burden** for couples. It is too difficult for many people to pay the price asked.

8   So, is lobola a rich tradition, bringing families together? Or is it an ugly custom of buying women? This debate continues in Botswana, as does the custom.

After You Read

LANGUAGE LEARNING STRATEGY

Identify arguments in your reading to help your understanding. Many readings present *arguments,* or ideas about which people disagree. Arguments are often presented in readings to help people understand the issues, and to make people think about their own opinion. When you identify arguments in your reading, you will understand the ideas more clearly.

Apply the Strategy

Review "Brides for Sale?" What are the arguments for lobola and against it? Fill in the chart with three or more arguments for and against lobola. One argument is done for you.

Arguments For	Arguments Against
Shows that families are coming together	

Which side do you agree with? Why? Discuss this with your class.

◆Vocabulary Building

With this ring I thee wed, with my body I thee worship, and with all my worldly goods I thee endow.

**—WEDDING VOW,
BOOK OF COMMON PRAYER**

Choose a word from this list that fits the clues in the questions.

asset	custom	individual
bride	debate	pride
cattle	generosity	rights
chores	groom	

1. These might include doing dishes, making the beds, and taking out the garbage: _____

2. This is another name for cows: _____

3. This means one person: _____

4. The couple in a wedding are the _____ and _____.

5. Something that is valuable is a/an _____.

6. This is another name for tradition: _____

7. Many parents think their sons and daughters should have these:

    _____

8. An argument is another name for this: _____

9. If you have strong positive feelings about your country and your traditions, you have this: _____

10. If your friends give you lots of gifts, they show their: _____

ACADEMIC POWER STRATEGY

Apply the Strategy

Organize your personal study space to improve your study sessions. Poor organization will make it difficult to study. If you can't find your books and notes, or you don't have a clean surface to work on, you will waste a lot of time. Get your workspace organized—this is a good step toward success.

1. Choose a quiet place.
2. Set up your desk or table with all of the tools you will need to study: paper, pens, pencils, highlighters, a stapler, a dictionary, a

(continued on next page)

trash basket and a good lamp. It might help to draw a plan. Use this space to plan where things should go. Draw in your desk, book cases, and any other important items:

3. Tell your family members or your roommate that this area is your study area. Ask them not to disturb you when you are working there.

4. Make it a habit to always study in this place. Creating and organizing your own study area will make you a more productive and successful student.

Grammar You Can Use

Adjectives and Adverbs

Adjectives and adverbs give us more information about nouns and verbs. For example, in the phrase, "a red house," the word "red" is an adjective, and describes "house," which is a noun. In the sentence, "He ate quickly," the word "ate" is a verb and "quickly" is an adverb that tells us about how he ate.

An important rule in using adjectives is that their form does not change. That is, you can have *three red books,* but not *three reds books.*

Often adverbs ends in *-ly,* so they are easy to identify. There are some words that end in *-ly* that are not adverbs, however: *lovely* and *friendly* are examples. Some adverbs don't have an *-ly* ending, either. *Well* and *fast* are examples.

Some words can be both adjectives and adverbs, such as *daily, monthly,* and *fast.*

In the following sentences, there are some mistakes in using adjectives and adverbs. Circle the word that is wrong, and rewrite the sentence correctly. Talk with your class about your answers.

1. She did good on her test. _____

   _____

2. He ran fastly to the store. _____

   _____

3. She has two blacks shoes. _____

   _____

4. She treated me friendly. _____

   _____

5. He works very careful. _____

   _____

Getting Ready to Read

Look at the definition of the word *dowry* below.

> **dow·ry** *noun* In some cultures, money or other valuables brought to a marriage by a woman.

What items do you think might be included in a dowry? List them here, and talk about them with your class.

_____

_____

Vocabulary Check

Look at the words and phrases below. Put a check mark next to the ones that you know. Talk with your class about the ones you don't know. Write the new words you learn in your Vocabulary Log.

———— banker   ———— hesitate

———— broaden my horizons   ———— in-laws

———— computerized   ———— linens

———— dowry   ———— necessities

———— grain   ———— professional

———— harsh   ———— VCRs

 Read

Reading 2: A New Dowry Item: The Computer

1   Min Huang is a **banker** in a small city in China. She surprised her new **in-laws** when she showed them a computer in her **dowry.** It was there with the traditional items like furniture, dishes, and **linens.**

2   When the family asked about the computer, she explained that she wanted to improve her **professional** skills. Her office had already been **computerized.**

3   "I also hope to connect to the Internet to **broaden my horizons,**" she said.

4   She told her parents that she wanted a computer for her dowry. They didn't **hesitate** to buy her one. They knew a computer would be important to her, and to her new family's future.

5   People who study Chinese marriage customs are very interested in this story. According to those customs, the groom's parents are responsible for the couple's housing. The bride's family supplies the daily **necessities.**

6   But, the contents of the dowry have changed over time. In the past, when rural people lived in fairly **harsh** conditions, they usually chose **grain** and clothing for a daughter who would soon be married. This showed their desire to protect her from hunger and cold.

7   In the 1950s, farm equipment and animals became popular items. Parents hoped that the daughter's life could be improved through hard work.

8   Modern times, however, bring the need for **VCRs,** stereos, and computers. Through these dowry items, parents hope that their daughter will be part of a successful, modern world.

9   Min's parents said, "We want our daughter to be a success. We want her to be part of a new world. A computer is part of that world."

10   Min completely agrees, and is thankful to have such generous and intelligent parents.

▸After You Read

1. What is a dowry?

2. What is Min Huang's job?

3. What items were included in Min Huang's dowry?

4. Why did she want a computer?

5. What will she do with her computer?

6. Why did her parents give her the computer?

7. According to Chinese tradition, what are the groom's parents responsible for?

8. What are the bride's parents responsible for?

9. What were some things included in dowries in the past?

10. What are some modern dowry items?

11. What does Min think of her parents?

12. Do you think the tradition of a dowry is a good one? Why or why not?

◆Vocabulary Building

1. Name three things in a modern **dowry**: _____, _____, and _____

2. Name two things in an old **dowry**: _____ and _____

3. Name two things that are considered **linens**: _____ and _____

4. Name two ways to **broaden your horizons**: _____ and _____

5. List three kinds of **in-laws**: _____, _____, and _____

6. Name three types of **grain**: _____, _____, and _____

7. List four **necessities** of life: _____, _____, _____, and _____

Test-Taking Tip

Use old tests to help study for a new one. Old tests can help you learn from past mistakes. You should always keep copies of your tests, if you can. Put them in a file folder or a safe place. Review your mistakes and reread anything you don't understand. Ask your instructor if you don't understand your mistakes.

You can also get copies of old tests from your current classes. Ask your instructor if you can have copies of tests from the past. Use these to help you study, too.

When you become familiar with old tests, you will feel more prepared to take new tests.

◆Getting Ready to Read

Love songs and love poems are popular in all cultures. Can you think of a love song or poem that you like from your native culture? Talk about this with your class. If you have a tape or CD of the song, bring it to class to share with everyone.

> **Love is not just looking at each other, it's looking in the same direction.**
>
> **—ANTOINE DE SAINT EXUPERY**

Vocabulary Check

Look at the words and phrases below. Put a check mark next to the ones that you know. Talk with your class about the ones you don't know. Write the new words you learn in your Vocabulary Log.

_____ character	_____ member	_____ syllables
_____ contests	_____ oral tradition	_____ theme
_____ embroideries	_____ praise (verb)	_____ verses
_____ back and forth	_____ receptions	_____ wisdom
_____ goodwill	_____ souvenirs	
_____ hardship	_____ strict	

 Read

Reading 3: Songs of Love on Crete

1   The people of Crete have a rich history that includes songs, dances, poetry, and much more. An important part of Cretan folk culture is the *mantinades*. These are colorful poems made up of two lines and exactly thirty **syllables.** They have been passed down for centuries through an **oral tradition.** They are filled with love and **wisdom.**

2   Mantinades probably started as love songs during the 1400s. Young people lived with **strict** rules in the Middle Ages. They weren't allowed to date. Their parents chose their marriage partners. So, these songs might have been used by lovers to send messages about secret meeting places.

3   Today, Cretans are proud of the mantinades. For generations, the songs have helped them express their history and feelings. The **verses** are about many different things, but most are about romantic love, **hardship,** and pride. They are often sung with a musical instrument called a *lyra*. They are an important part of wedding **receptions** on Crete.

4   At large weddings, there are often friendly **contests.** At a wedding, the guests might divide into two groups and sit at tables facing each other. They then hold a contest: one **member** from each side sings a mantinade. The last seven syllables are repeated by the other side before beginning a new verse.

5   Both sides sing verses about one **theme** as they try to do better than the other. They go **back and forth** until the "losers" have run out of mantinades.

6   The mantinades at wedding celebrations show the **goodwill** of the Cretan people. In the contests, many of the verses **praise** the good looks and **character** of the bride and groom. Others give advice and blessings. Some talk about the couple's future children.

7   The mantinades also express feelings about various marriage customs, such as the dowry. The verses sometimes make fun of the importance of choosing a bride with a large dowry. These dowries include property and traditional **embroideries** that the bride's mother has been sewing since the bride was born. Other verses express the unhappiness of young women married off to older men.

8   Some think that in recent years the verses have become political and commercial. In fact, political writers often use the mantinades. They are often found on **souvenirs,** like calendars and ashtrays, too. But most Cretans aren't worried. The verses sung at weddings come from the rich memory of the people of Crete. Old and young alike share a love for poetry and for Cretan history. Most believe that the mantinades will live for many more generations.

◆**After You Read**

1. Where is Crete?

2. What are the mantinades?

3. How do people learn mantinades?

4. How did mantinades begin?

5. What are these poems about?

6. How are mantinades used at weddings?

7. What feelings are expressed in wedding mantinades?

8. What are some new places where mantinades can be found?

9. Are the Cretans worried about the future of the mantinades? Why or why not?

10. What is your opinion of the mantinades?

◆Vocabulary Building

Complete the paragraph using the words from this list. Cross off words as you use them.

character	hardship	syllables
contest	oral tradition	themes
back and forth	receptions	verse
goodwill		

A mantinade is a song or _____ sung on the island of Crete. It has exactly 30 _____. It is part of the _____ of Crete. At wedding _____, the mantinades are sung to praise the _____ of the bride and groom. They show the _____ of the guests. Often, there is a _____ and the guests sing mantinades _____ until one side wins. Mantinades have many _____. Some express the _____ of life, but most are happy songs. Mantinades are an important part of Cretan culture.

TUNING IN:
"Marriage & Family Therapists"

Before you watch the video, look at the following words. Put a check mark next to the words or phrases that you know. Talk with your class about the ones you don't know. Write the new words you learn in your Vocabulary Log.

© CNN

———— behave

———— counseling

———— eating disorder

———— insurance

———— mental health professionals

———— psychosis

———— rebuilding

———— sessions

———— severe

———— therapist

Watch "Marriage & Family Therapists" and fill in the missing numbers in the chart.

Satisfied	———————— %
Relations improved	Nearly ———————— %
———————— % of cases	———————— sessions

What does the information in this chart show? Talk about this question with your classmates. Watch the video again and answer these questions:

1. How did marriage and family therapy help Nancy Leving?

2. Why don't all mental health professionals like marriage and family therapists?

3. How many marriage and family therapists are there?

4. How much does it cost to go to a marriage and family therapist?

Getting Ready to Read

The next reading talks about magic and superstition, as they relate to wedding traditions. Talk with your class about these questions:

1. Where do traditions come from?

2. What is *superstition?*

3. Describe some superstitions you know about.

4. Are you superstitious? Why or why not?

Vocabulary Check

Look at the following words and phrases. Put a check mark next to the ones that you know. Talk with your class about the ones you don't know. Write the new words you learn in your Vocabulary Log.

I love thee, I love but thee
    With a love that shall not die
    Till the sun grows cold,
    And the stars grow old . . .

—WILLIAM SHAKESPEARE

_____ ancient   _____ smashing

_____ candles   _____ superstitions

_____ demons   _____ the Middle Ages

_____ envy   _____ torches

_____ evil spirits   _____ traces

_____ lamps   _____ veil

_____ magical   _____ warned

_____ medieval   _____ wedding marches

_____ scared

Read

Reading 4: The Magic in Marriage

1 Over the centuries, Jewish people have lived in many different countries. Because of this, they have taken on the customs of the people around them and added them to their own. Many of today's traditional Jewish wedding customs have this kind of history.

2   One common belief shared by many people in **ancient** times was a belief in **demons** or **evil spirits.** They believed that these spirits tried to attack people, especially at times of happiness, such as marriage. We find some **traces** of these beliefs even today in Jewish weddings as well as other types of weddings.

3   The joy of a wedding was believed to bring anger and **envy** to the spirit world. Therefore, many marriage customs began as protection for the bride and groom. For example, the Jewish bride wears a **veil** to protect her from the "evil eye." This custom is common in other cultures, too.

4   Ancient people also believed that fire and light **scared** demons. Therefore, the **wedding marches** in old cultures included **lamps, candles** or **torches.** This custom is still part of many Jewish weddings today. The ceremony often includes candles.

5   The _chuppah_ (bridal canopy) is a traditional part of most Jewish weddings. This covering was spread above the couple to protect them from attacks by demons.

6   The Near East is the source of the Jewish tradition of **smashing** a glass at the end of the ceremony. Smashing glasses or dishes was a common **magical** practice in the Near East. It represented smashing the powers of demons and anyone who did not wish the couple well. (This practice is still common today. However, sometimes a light bulb is broken instead, because it is safer than breaking a glass.)

7   In **medieval** Germany, the marriage glass was often thrown against a special stone, which was part of the northern wall of a Jewish temple. The ancient Jews believed that demons came down from the north. By smashing a glass on this stone, they smashed it in the face of the demons. By doing this, they hoped to get rid of their evil wishes.

8   Most of these customs, of course, are **superstitions.** Tradition **warned** Jewish people not to believe in superstitions. However, the attitude of European Jews in **the Middle Ages** is shown in a popular 13th-century German-Jewish book. It says, "One should not believe in superstitions, but it is good to be careful of them."

After You Read

1. Where do many Jewish wedding traditions come from, according to the reading?

2. What is a demon?

3. How did many wedding traditions begin?

4. Why does a Jewish bride traditionally wear a veil?

5. Why do Jewish weddings often include candles or lamps?

6. What is a bridal canopy? What does it do?

7. Why is a glass smashed at the end of a Jewish wedding?

8. What does the saying at the end of the reading mean?

9. Do you know of other cultures that believe in the "evil eye"?

◆**Vocabulary Building**

Put these words into categories below. Some words might fit into more than one category.

ancient	envy	magical	smashing glass
candles	evil spirits	medieval	torches
demons	lamps	scared	veil

Things you might see at a wedding	Words related to feelings at weddings	Words related to superstition

LANGUAGE LEARNING STRATEGY

Identify the main idea of your readings. Often, readings contain a lot of ideas and many examples and details. How can you tell what the *main* idea is? Here are some ways:

- Look for key words that are repeated. These are often related to the main idea.

- Review the topic sentences. (Review the Language Learning Strategy about topic sentences on page 72.) These usually relate to the main idea.

- Read the introduction and conclusion carefully. These usually state the main idea.

Apply the Strategy

On the next page there is a list of main ideas, which appear in the readings in this chapter. Draw a line to the reading each fits best.

(continued on next page)

1. Brides for Sale?	a. Some traditions keep up with modern times.
2. A New Dowry Item: The Computer	b. Many wedding traditions are based on old superstitions.
3. Magic in Marriage	c. An old tradition provides happiness at weddings.
4. Songs of Love on Crete	d. Some wedding traditions are controversial, and should be discussed.

PUTTING IT ALL TOGETHER

> There is nothing nobler or more admirable than when two people who see eye to eye keep house as man and wife, confounding their enemies and delighting their friends.
>
> —HOMER, *ODYSSEY*

There are several traditions in North American weddings that cause disagreement. There are also some traditions in this chapter that are controversial. With a group of classmates, organize a debate about one of these topics.

1. Should wives promise to obey their husbands in their wedding vows?

2. Should fathers "give away" their daughters as part of the wedding ceremony?

3. Should wives be expected to have a dowry?

4. Should parents arrange marriages?

5. Fill in another tradition you think is debatable: _____

_____

Each debate team should prepare their arguments ahead of time. Try to guess what the other side's arguments will be. Fill out this table to help you organize:

Arguments for _____	Arguments against _____

The organization of the debate should go like this:

Side 1: Opening statement, 1 minute

Side 2: Opening statement, 1 minute

Side 1: Main arguments, 2 minutes

Side 2: Main arguments, 2 minutes

Side 1: Discussion of Side 2's arguments, 2 minutes

Side 2: Discussion of Side 1's arguments, 2 minutes

Side 1: Closing statement, 2 minutes

Side 2: Closing statement, 2 minutes

At the end of the debate, everyone in class should vote on which side won the debate.

CHECK YOUR PROGRESS

On a scale of 1 to 5, rate how well you've mastered the goals set at the beginning of the chapter:

1 2 3 4 5   identify arguments in your reading.

1 2 3 4 5   identify the main idea in your reading.

1 2 3 4 5   organize your study area.

1 2 3 4 5   use old tests to help study for new ones.

1 2 3 4 5   understand adverbs and adjectives.

If you've given yourself a 3 or lower on any of these goals:

- visit the *Tapestry* web site for additional practice.

- ask your instructor for extra help.

- review the sections of the chapter that you found difficult.

- work with a partner or study group to further your progress.

L ook at the photo. It is of three characters from Greek mythology: Orpheus, Eurydice, and Hermes. Talk about these questions with your class:

- What kinds of stories are myths?
- Have you heard of any Greek myths?
- Why are myths important to people?

TELLING STORIES

This chapter looks at stories called myths, which are important in many cultures. Myths tell the important stories of a culture. In this chapter, you will read about the myth represented in the photo, as well as myths from Japan, North America, and Africa.

Setting Goals

In this chapter, you will learn how to:

◈ understand plagiarism.

◈ take notes on a reading.

◈ make a character chart.

◈ cram for a test.

◈ use participles as adjectives.

Which goal is most important to you?_____

_____

Why?_____

Talk about your answers with your class.

◆Getting Started

With a group of classmates, try to think of stories about the world's beginning. How many different stories of how the world began does your group know? Make a list of them.

◆Getting Ready to Read

This reading defines the words *myth* and *mythology*. Skim the reading (review the strategy of skimming on page 52), and write down the main ideas here. Take only two minutes to skim the reading:

The Muses are mythological goddesses who are said to give artists their ideas and inspiration.

1. What is this reading about? _____
_____

2. What is a myth? _____
_____

3. Why are myths important? _____
_____

Vocabulary Check

Look at the words below. Put a check mark next to the words that you know. Talk with your class about the words you don't know. Write the new words you learn in your Vocabulary Log.

_____ anthropology	_____ entertain	_____ reason
_____ archaeology	_____ fairy tales	_____ seeds
_____ blacksmith	_____ foundation	_____ supernatural
_____ complicated	_____ psychology	_____ urban
_____ disciplines		

◆Read

Reading 1: Myths and Mythology

What is a Myth?
. . . .

1　The word *myth* doesn't have one single definition, but many different ones. However, in general, a myth is a **complicated** cultural story. It describes the beginnings and other basic parts of a culture. Myths tell, for example, how the world began, how people and animals were created, and how certain customs started.

2　Myths are not the same as **fairy tales**. Myths usually talk about a time before history, or before the world began. They are more serious and more **supernatural** than fairy tales. Their purpose is not only to **entertain** people, but to teach them about the **foundation** of a culture.

3　Myths are often thought of as religious stories, because they talk about gods and other supernatural beings. However, myths go beyond religious beliefs. Therefore, they can tell us about many parts of human life and culture, not just religion.

What is Mythology?

4 Mythology is the study and explanation of myths. For example, people who study Greek mythology study how myth is in conflict with **reason.** Others study the similarities and differences between the myths of different cultures.

What are the Types of Myth?

5 Myths can be categorized into the types of themes they talk about. Here are some examples of those themes:

6 **The World's Beginning:** Usually, the most important myth in a culture tells how the world began. In some stories, such as in the first chapter of the Bible, the creation of the world begins from nothing. Other stories say the world has different levels. Another kind of creation story talks about the world having parents. In the Babylonian story, the parents, Apsu and Tiamat, have children who later battle their parents. The children win the fight, and the world is created from the body of Tiamat.

7 **The World's End:** Myths about the end of the world usually come from **urban** societies. They tell about the creation of the world by a god,

who also destroys the world. At the end of the world, people are judged and prepared for heaven or hell. In Aztec[1] mythology, several worlds are created and destroyed by the gods before the beginning of the human world.

8 **Creation of Nature:** Many myths tell how animals were created. For example, many Native American myths tell stories of animals being made out of natural materials, such as wood or stone.

9 **Cultural Heroes:** Myths of cultural heroes tell of beings that discovered important ideas or things. For example, in Greek mythology, Prometheus stole fire from the gods. In the African Dogon culture, a **blacksmith** stole **seeds** from the gods so that people could grow food with the seeds.

Who Studies Mythology?

10 Researchers in many fields study mythology. Some study myths themselves with information from history, **archaeology, anthropology,** and other **disciplines.** Others use myths to study ideas in their fields—in **psychology,** for example.

11 Many people are interested in mythology because it helps us understand culture and history throughout the world. Even though myths are stories from before ancient times, people in modern times are very curious about these stories, too. They are interested in what myths can teach us today.

[1]The Aztecs were an ancient culture from the region that is now Mexico. They built pyramids and had other sophisticated inventions, such as calendars and water systems.

LANGUAGE LEARNING STRATEGY

Take notes on a reading to help your understanding of the reading. Taking notes on a reading allows you to keep track of important information while you read and helps you to check that you have understood what you have read. When you take notes on a reading, you can write down the important definitions, concepts, or events.

You should organize your notes so that they are easy to read when you review them for a test. One way to write notes is to put the name of the important word, topic concept, or event on one side of the paper and the definition, example, or explanation on the other side of the paper. It might look like this:

Topic 1	First example
	Second example
Topic 2	First example
	Second example

Apply the Strategy

Reread "Myths and Mythology," this time taking notes as you read. Compare your notes with a partner's notes. Did you write down the same information?

 **After You Read**

Review your notes before you talk about these questions:

1. What is a myth?

2. What is mythology?

3. Who studies mythology?

4. How are fairy tales different from myths?

5. What are some themes that myths talk about?

6. Who was Prometheus?

7. Why are people interested in mythology?

Vocabulary Building

Cross out the word in each line that does *not* mean the same thing as the others. The first one is done for you.

> The Furies were mythological spirits. They punished people who committed crimes against their own families.

1. battle   fight   ~~meeting~~   combat
2. complicated   different   complex   tangled
3. blame   condemn   warn   criticize
4. disorder   field   area   discipline
5. entertain   bore   amuse   delight
6. foundation   base   structure   groundwork
7. believer   thinker   philosopher   theorist
8. reason   logic   thought   common sense
9. religion   faith   belief   history
10. supernatural mythical   white   ghostly
11. urban   city   civic   rural

Test-Taking Tip

Learn to cram effectively for your tests (but avoid cramming whenever you can). Cramming means studying very hard right before a test. It is not the best way to study. However, almost every student finds he or she needs to cram occasionally. Here are some tips for more effective cramming:

- Don't try to learn everything. Choose a few things to study well.
- Recite and repeat. Keep going over the facts until you know them perfectly.
- Remember to use your notes, flash cards, and review sheets.
- Cram with a study group. Drill each other on questions and answers.
- Relax. Cramming often makes people nervous. Try to relax when you have to cram.

Remember, it is best to plan and study in advance, in order to avoid cramming. But, when you have to cram, make a plan and do your best.

◆**Getting Ready to Read**

This reading tells a Native American myth. Before you read, write in your journal about Native Americans. How much do you already know? You can start by answering these questions:

1. Have you seen Native Americans in movies or on TV? Describe what you have seen.

2. Have you read about Native Americans? Write down what you remember.

3. Can you think of any famous Native Americans? Name them.

4. Write anything else you know or think of when you hear the phrase "Native American."

Vocabulary Check

Look at the words and phrases below. Put a check mark next to the ones that you know. Talk with your class about the ones you don't know. Write the new words you learn in your Vocabulary Log.

_____ achievement	_____ magnificent	_____ scales
_____ body of water	_____ masterpiece	_____ spirits
_____ copper	_____ polished	
_____ crane	_____ pounded	

◆**Read**

Reading 2: Awasassi: An Ojibwe Folktale

Nanaboozhou (nan-a-BOO-zhew) is half spirit and half human. One day, he decided to help out the Great Spirit by making all of the fish. When he finished with all but the last fish, Nanaboozhou ran out of **scales.** He transformed himself into a **crane** and took long steps up to the Keweenaw Peninsula[1] of Michigan, where the Anishinabe (first people) got raw **copper.** Nanaboozhou **pounded** some of this copper into flat, round scales and **polished** them with fine sand from the beach. When he finished lining up the scales on this last, beautiful fish, he realized that he had cre-

[1] A peninsula is a piece of land that is surrounded on three sides by water.

ated a **masterpiece.** Nanaboozhou completed his **achievement** by giving this fish a beautiful voice as well.

Called Awasassi, the bull-head,[2] this fish was placed in all of the streams, lakes, and rivers of the North Woods. At each **body of water,** Nanaboozhou held the **magnificent** creature out to each of the four directions and asked the **spirits** to bless her. Then Nanaboozhou leaned far out and gently lowered Awasassi into the cool water.

Source: *Cobblestone,* November 1998 Vol. 19, #8

After You Read

1. Who is Nanaboozhou?

2. Why did he decide to make all the fish?

3. How did he make the fish?

4. What kind of fish did he make?

5. What is copper?

6. Where does this myth take place?

7. Review the types of myths listed in "Myths and Mythology." What is the theme of this myth?

Vocabulary Building

Write the correct word or phrase in the blank.

a body of water	polish	scales
crane	pound	a spirit
a masterpiece	copper	transformed

1. The Pacific Ocean is one of these: _____

2. These are found on a fish's skin: _____

3. This is a type of metal: _____

4. This is a type of bird: _____

5. A painting by Van Gogh or Picasso might be called this:

   _____

6. Another word for *changed* is _____

7. A being that is not human or animal might be this:

   _____

8. You can use a hammer to do this: _____

9. When you do this to something, you make it shiny:

   _____

[2]A bull-head is a type of large-headed, North American freshwater catfish.

ACADEMIC POWER STRATEGY

Understand your school's rules about plagiarism. Different cultures have different attitudes about plagiarism. It is important to understand the attitude of the culture in which you are studying.

Plagiarism is using the work of someone else and claiming that it is your own. For example, the story about Awasassi comes from the magazine *Cobblestone*, Nov. 1998 Vol. 19, #8. If that information was not written at the end of the story, the readers of this book would assume that the authors of this book wrote the story about Awasassi. This is not true, since the story of Awasassi is an ancient Ojibwe folktale. In order to avoid plagiarism, the information about where the story comes from must be included.

As a student, anytime you use exact words from a story or other reading, you must put quotation marks (" ") around those words, and you must tell where you got the information you are using. Knowing about your school's policy on plagiarism will help you avoid being accused of dishonesty.

Apply the Strategy

Find out your school's policy on plagiarism. Answer these questions:

1. Where can you find your school's policy on plagiarism?

2. What are the penalties for plagiarism?

3. How can you avoid plagiarism in your work?

TUNING IN: "Totem Poles"

© CNN

In this video, you will see three places related to totem poles and to Native American traditions. These places are listed in the columns on the next page. As you watch, place the following words in the column of the place where you see the objects. You may use the words more than once.

cedar totems	The Raven and the First Men
fire	tourists
jewelry	wooden building
photographers	woods
sweat lodge	

STANLEY PARK	MUSEUM OF ANTHROPOLOGY	A SHORT DISTANCE FROM THE MUSEUM
_____	_____	_____
_____	_____	_____
_____	_____	_____
_____	_____	_____

Now answer these questions about the video with your class:

1. What are the four functions of the totem poles?

2. What is the story of "The Raven and the First Men"?

3. What is the sweat lodge? Why are many people invited to the sweat lodge now?

Getting Ready to Read

In the last reading, Nanaboozhou changed himself into a crane. In this reading, the same animal appears in Japanese mythology. Look at the photo of a crane below.

1. Write a short description of the crane. Talk about your description with your class.

2. Find more information about cranes on the Internet or in your library. Answer these questions:

   - Where do cranes live?

   - How big are they?

   - Are there different kinds of cranes?

   - Are cranes endangered?

Talk about what you found out with your class.

Vocabulary Check

Look at the following words and phrases. Put a check mark next to the ones that you know. Talk with your class about the ones you don't know. Write the new words you learn in your Vocabulary Log.

_____ gratitude   _____ released   _____ to slip away

_____ mask   _____ roll   _____ wove

_____ midnight   _____ snare

Read

Reading 3: A Japanese Myth: "The Crane"

1   A long time ago, a crane fell in the snow in the mountains. She was caught in a **snare.** A young man who was walking in the mountains found the crane. He saw that she was caught in a snare, so he **released** her and she flew away.

2   A few days later, a beautiful woman visited the young man's house at **midnight.** She told him that she had lost her way in the mountains. She asked him if she could stay at his house that night. The young man, who fell in love with her at first sight, said she could stay.

3   To show her **gratitude,** the beautiful woman **wove** a thick **roll** of fine brocade.[1] Night after night, she stayed at the young man's house and wove the material. He sold it in the market place and became very rich.

4   But the beautiful woman never let the young man watch her when she was weaving. The young man became more and more curious, until one night, he broke into the room. In the room, he saw a crane weaving with her feathers. He was very shocked! He tried **to slip away,** but the crane saw him. She said, "Until now, I could wear the **mask** of a beautiful woman. I did it because I loved you. But now that you know I am a crane, I must leave you."

5   The young man cried out, "Don't leave! Please come back!"

6   But the crane flew away into the evening sky with tears in her eyes and she never came back.

—_Traditional Japanese myth as told to the author by Noriko Oguma_

After You Read

1. Where did the young man find the crane?

2. What did he do for her?

3. Why did the woman come to the man's house?

4. What did she make for him?

5. Why couldn't he watch her weave the cloth?

6. Why did she leave him?

[1]Brocade is a type of cloth that has a pattern on it made with heavy thread.

7. Do you know any other stories like this one?

8. Is this story more like a fairy tale or a myth? Explain your answer.

Vocabulary Building

Write the correct word in the blanks of the paragraph.

brocade	mask	roll	slipped away
gratitude	midnight	shocked	wove
lost her way	released	snare	

A crane was caught in a _____. A young man _____ her. Later, a woman appeared at his door at _____. She said she had _____. He was _____ to see her there. She wanted to show her _____. So, she _____ him a thick _____ of _____. She never let him watch her weaving. But, one night he saw her. He discovered she was a crane wearing a _____. She _____ and left him forever.

Grammar You Can Use

Participles

Participles are words that are made from verbs, but can be used as types of adjectives. Participles are made by adding *-ing* or *-ed*. Look at these examples:

> That is an *exciting* myth.

> The *bored* student fell asleep in class.

When do you use *-ing* and when do you use *-ed?* With the words *bore* and *excite,* think about these sentences:

> The lecture was *boring* so I felt *bored.*

> The movie was *exciting* so I felt *excited.*

If you say, "*I am boring,*" it means that other people fall asleep when you talk. If you say, "*I am exciting,*" some people might think you are bragging.

Write the correct form of the participle in the blank on the following page. The base form is given in parentheses at the beginning of the sentence. The first one is done for you.

1. (bore) I almost fell asleep in the movie because I was __bored__.

2. (shock) The young man was _____ when he saw the crane.

3. (entertain) The movie was very _____.

4. (complicate) The story of the Greek myth is very _____.

5. (transform) After hearing the story, he was a _____ man.

6. (polish) The _____ stone was beautiful.

Could any of these sentences use both forms? Why or why not?

Getting Ready to Read

Talk about these questions with your class:

1. What is humility? If you don't know this word, look it up in your dictionary.

2. Is it important to be humble? Why or why not?

3. What happens to people who are not humble, in your opinion?

4. Do you know any stories or sayings about humility?

The Sirens were mythological bird-women who attracted sailors with song. The sailors usually died, because they jumped into the sea to live with the Sirens.

Vocabulary Check

Look at the words below. Put a check mark next to the words that you know. Talk with your class about the ones you don't know. Write the new words you learn in your Vocabulary Log.

_____ arrested	_____ goddess	_____ soldiers
_____ bumped	_____ humility	_____ spilled
_____ consulted	_____ perplexed	_____ stained
_____ crossroads	_____ robes	

Read

Reading 4: Nigerian Myth: "Obatala Visits Shango"

1 One day, Obatala, The Chief of the White Cloth, decided to visit his son Shango, the god of fire who lived in another city. First, he **consulted** Ifa', a system of divination.[1] Ifa' said that Obatala must learn the lesson of **humility** before visiting his son Shango. Obatala was confident that he already knew the lesson of humility, so he decided to start the journey to visit his son.

[1]*Divination* is a way of finding things out through magic.

2   On the journey, Obatala met Ellegua, the god of the **cross-roads.** Ellegua was getting ready to carry a jar of red palm oil.[2] When he saw Obatala coming, he asked Obatala to help him place the jar of oil on his head. Obatala picked up the jar, but Ellegua **bumped** the jar and **spilled** red oil all over Obatala's white **robes.**

3   Obatala decided to wash the red oil out of his robes, so he went to the river. Obatala realized that the red oil had **stained** his eyes, so he took out his eyes and cleaned them in the river. Then he placed his eyes on a rock and began to wash his clothes. Ellegua, who had followed Obatala to the river, stole Obatala's eyes and gave them to Oshun, the river **goddess.**

4   Obatala, who was now blind, began to search for his eyes, and he went to Oshun, the river goddess. Oshun told Obatala that she would return his eyes if Obatala would teach her divination. Obatala agreed. Oshun learned the secrets of divination on that day and shared those secrets with all of the other gods and goddesses.

5   Now that he had his eyes back, Obatala started again on his journey to see his son. He was **perplexed** by everything that had happened to him. As he got closer to his son's city, he saw a wild horse coming at him. He jumped up on the horse and stopped it, but the **soldiers** of the city **arrested** Obatala because they thought he was a horse thief. They threw Obatala in jail. In the jail, Obatala thought about the lesson of humility.

6   When Shango heard that his father was in jail, he immediately came to ask for forgiveness and ordered the soldiers to release Obatala. Obatala greeted Shango and then returned home without saying a word.

—Traditional Nigerian Myth

 **After You Read**

1. Where did Obatala want to go?

2. What did Obatala learn from Ifa'?

3. What happened when Obatala met Ellegua?

4. What happened when Obatala met Oshun?

5. Why was Obatala arrested?

6. Why did Obatala leave without saying a word?

7. Did Obatala really know the lesson of humility before his journey? Why or why not?

8. What lessons have you learned "on a journey"?

A lyre is an old musical instrument with strings, like a small guitar.

[2]Palm oil is oil taken from palm trees.

LANGUAGE LEARNING STRATEGY

Make a character chart to help you understand and remember the different characters in a story. When you make a character chart, put the name of the character in one column and the important information about that character in another column. For example, here is a character chart for the myth "Awasassi: An Ojibwe Folktale":

Character	Important Information
Nanaboozhou	half spirit and half human created Awasassi
Awasassi	bull-head fish very beautiful had scales of copper

When you make a character chart, you have all of the important information about a character in one place. This will help you study and remember the characters in a story.

Apply the Strategy

Make a character chart for "Obatala Visits Shango."

◀ Getting Ready to Read

At the beginning of the chapter you saw a photo of Orpheus and Eurydice. The next reading tells their story. Before you read it, find this information (*hint* for questions 2, 3, 4, and 5: review the **Threads** in this chapter):

1. Find Thrace, an area of Ancient Greece, on the map on the next page.

2. What is a Muse? _____

3. What are Sirens? _____

4. Who are the Furies? _____

5. What is a *lyre*? _____

Vocabulary Check

Look at the words below. Put a check mark next to the ones that you know. Talk with your class about the words you don't know. Write the new words you learn in your Vocabulary Log.

_____ beloved   _____ dishonest   _____ reputation

_____ blink   _____ drown out   _____ residents

_____ crushed   _____ melted   _____ taming

Read

Reading 5: Orpheus and Eurydice

1 Orpheus was a great Thracian[1] hero. He was the son of king Oeager and the Muse Calliope. He was famous throughout Greece because of his skills in music and poetry.

2   During the voyage of Jason's ship, the Argo, the songs of Orpheus could even **drown out** the song of the Sirens. Before that, the song of the Sirens was deadly to all the travelers who heard it.

3   Orpheus was even successful in **taming** Hades, the god of the Underworld.[2] According to the myth, his **beloved** wife Eurydice died young after being bitten by a snake. Orpheus went down into the Underworld to

---

[1]*Thracian* means a person from the city of Thrace.

[2]The Underworld refers to a place below the surface of the earth where the land of Hades was. It was considered an evil place.

bring her back. The sound of Orpheus' lyre **melted** the hearts of all the **residents** of the dark Underworld.

4   Cerberus, the hated dog of Hell, lay down peacefully for the first time. The suffering of those being punished stopped for a while. Even the terrible Furies began to cry.

5   Hades was very pleased. He told Orpheus that he could take his wife back with him. However, Orpheus was not allowed to turn around to look at her until he was back in the land of the living. So, the couple left in silence. Before they left the gates of the Underworld, Orpheus suddenly began to doubt the honesty of Hades. Hades had a **reputation** as a **dishonest** character. So, Orpheus turned around to check that Eurydice really was following him.

6   In a **blink** of an eye, she was gone forever. Orpheus was **crushed** by the loss of his beloved wife. He died shortly after.

After You Read

1. Who is Orpheus?

2. Who is Eurydice?

3. Who is Hades?

4. How did Eurydice die?

5. Why did Orpheus go to the Underworld?

6. Why did Hades allow Orpheus to take Eurydice back with him?

7. What rule did Orpheus have to follow?

8. Why did he break the rule?

9. How does the story end?

10. Many myths, like this one, have different versions, with different endings. Look at the two different versions of this myth's ending:

Ending 1: Some of the gods of Thrace tore Orpheus apart and scattered his pieces, because he had shown disrespect for the mysteries of the gods.

Ending 2: Orpheus was killed by the god Zeus, for later revealing the mysteries of the gods to humans.

a. Which ending do you prefer? Why?

b. What are the lessons of each of the endings?

Vocabulary Building

Complete each sentence. Show that you understand the meaning of the word in **bold**.

1. If someone is **beloved,** _____.

2. You feel **crushed** if _____.

3. It is **dishonest** to _____.

4. The _____ was **drowned out** by the noise.

5. My friend has a _____ **reputation**

   because _____.

6. It is hard to **tame** a _____.

PUTTING IT ALL TOGETHER

Create a collection of myths from people in your class. Each student should write a myth that he or she knows. Write it in the following form:

Name of Myth:

Country:

Put the story of the myth here.

Include a picture if you think the story needs one.

Collect all the myths in a notebook. If you can, make copies for each student. Talk about the stories you collected.

CHECK YOUR PROGRESS

On a scale of 1 to 5, rate how well you've mastered the goals set at the beginning of the chapter:

1 2 3 4 5   understand plagiarism.

1 2 3 4 5   take notes on a reading.

1 2 3 4 5   make a character chart.

1 2 3 4 5   cram for a test.

1 2 3 4 5   use participles as adjectives.

If you've given yourself a 3 or lower on any of these goals:

- visit the *Tapestry* web site for additional practice.

- ask your instructor for extra help.

- review the sections of the chapter that you found difficult.

- work with a partner or study group to further your progress.

L ook at the photo. Talk about these questions with your class:

- What is happening in this photo?
- Do you enjoy shopping?
- What is customer service?
- Do you think customer service is important?

BUYER BEWARE

Nearly everyone needs to shop. We need clothes, food, and other items in order to live. However, some people don't enjoy shopping. They complain that the service is bad, the prices are high, and it's difficult to find what they want. Others, of course, love shopping—they like the social activity and the opportunity to see new things. This chapter looks at shopping—new trends and some problems.

Setting Goals

In this chapter, you will learn how to:

◈ write summaries to help you understand a reading.

◈ understand the difference between fact and opinion.

◈ plan enough time to complete assignments.

◈ use your journal to help with tests.

◈ remember irregular verb forms.

Which goal is most important to you?_____

_____

Why?_____

Talk about your answers with your class.

◆**Getting Started**

Preview this chapter, then answer these questions:

1. Which title looks most interesting to you?

2. Why?

3. Do you already know something about these things? Check the ones you know about.

_____ a. customer service   _____ c. Internet shopping

_____ b. shopping malls   _____ d. freedom of speech

Explain what you know to a partner.

◆**Getting Ready to Read**

Before you read "Shopping in Little Saigon, Texas," with a group of classmates, make a list of the kinds of shops you usually find in malls.

Vocabulary Check

Look at the words and phrases below. Put a check mark next to the ones that you know. Talk with your class about the words and phrases you don't know. Write the new words you learn in your Vocabulary Log.

_____ census   _____ Laotian   _____ specialties

_____ estimates (noun) _____ loan   _____ travel agency

_____ hair salon   _____ mall   _____ vacant

_____ jewelry   _____ real estate   _____ Vietnamese

◆**Read**

Reading 1: Shopping in Little Saigon, Texas

1 In Haltom City, near Dallas, Texas, a new shopping **mall** has opened. It's called the Little Saigon Mall. There is a large grocery store, which offers Asian **specialties** and other foods. There are also several small shops that feature **Vietnamese** goods.

2   Business is excellent. The parking lot is nearly full. One thousand customers eat lunch or dinner each day at the mall's new Vietnamese restaurant. This noodle soup restaurant just opened at the mall.

3   There are a large number of Vietnamese and **Laotian** residents living in Haltom City. More than 48,000 Asian and Pacific-Islanders live in the county, according to **estimates** from the regional **census**. The owner of the supermarket, Mr. Dang, said

he is delighted that local residents now have another place to shop, eat, and meet with friends.

4   In addition to the restaurant, the Little Saigon Mall contains a **hair salon**, a video and gift shop, a **jewelry** store, a **loan** company, and a coffee shop. The owners of these stores say they've had a lot of customers since the mall opened.

5   "Many years ago, we didn't have places to go," said the coffee shop's owner. "We just went to work or stayed home."

6   One large space is still **vacant** inside the mall. Mr. Dang said he would like a clothing store, **travel agency**, doctor's office, or **real estate** office to move into the empty area.

7   Customers come from all over the Dallas area. You don't have to be Vietnamese to enjoy the mall, of course. Sara Martin, a Dallas resident, said she stops at the mall nearly every day on her way home from work. "Everything is easy to find," she said. "The prices are good and the food is very fresh."

 **After You Read**

1. Where is the city of Saigon?

2. Where is the Little Saigon Mall?

3. What kinds of shops are at the mall?

4. Are the businesses there doing well? Give some examples.

5. How many Asians and Pacific-Islanders live in the area of the mall?

6. What kind of store does Mr. Dang want to move into the mall?

7. What kinds of shoppers visit the mall?

8. Would you enjoy shopping at this mall? Why or why not?

◆Vocabulary Building

Fill in the blanks with the words from this list:

census   loan company   travel agency

hair salon   real estate   vacant

jewelry store   specialties   Vietnamese

Laotian

1. Name two adjectives related to Asian countries: _____
   and _____

2. This word means empty: _____

3. Name five kinds of businesses that might be found in a mall:
   _____ , _____ , _____ ,
   _____ , and _____

4. This is the official count of a population: _____

5. The grocery store sells these: Asian _____

ACADEMIC POWER STRATEGY

Plan enough time to complete your assignments. Planning is very important in all your work. For example, if you use a computer to write your papers, plan to finish your essay a day or two before it is due. This way, if you have problems printing your work, you will have time to fix the problem. Also, plan time to make one final check of your work before you give it to your instructor. When you plan enough time to complete your assignments, you avoid extra stress, too.

Apply the Strategy

Answer these questions:

1. What assignments do you have that are due in the next two weeks?
   List them here:

   _____

   _____

   _____

   _____

2. How long will it take you to complete them?

_____

_____

3. How much time can you leave to avoid problems?

_____

_____

4. Share your plans in a group of three or four students.

5. Write suggestions or ideas you get from talking with these students.

_____

_____

_____

_____

◄Getting Ready to Read

Before you read "Malls: Public Places or Private Businesses?" talk about these questions with your class:

1. What is free speech?

2. Do Americans have the right to free speech everywhere?

3. Do you know what the exceptions to free speech are?

4. Have you ever been asked to sign a petition at a mall?

Vocabulary Check

Look at the words below. Put a check mark next to the words that you know. Talk with your class about the words you don't know. Write the new words you learn in your Vocabulary Log.

_____ arrested	_____ demonstrations	_____ pleaded
_____ charge	_____ dismissed	_____ represents
_____ charity	_____ fundraisers	_____ suburbs
_____ constitution	_____ hire	_____ sweatshops
_____ crime	_____ leaflets	_____ violated

The largest mall in the United States is the Mall of America in Bloomington, Minnesota. The mall is 4.2 million square feet, has 400 shops, 12,000 employees, and includes a seven-acre amusement park.

Read

Reading 2: Malls: Public Places or Private Businesses?

1   Three young men were **arrested** at an Iowa shopping mall. They didn't steal anything. Their **crime**: handing out information about **sweatshops,** places that use workers illegally. The shopping center says it doesn't allow **demonstrations.** That's why they were arrested.

2   Many people were upset about the arrests. They say the shopping mall is trying to stop freedom of speech.

3   The mall owner says the protestors were on private property. Free speech doesn't apply there. The security guards asked the protesters to leave. Two of them did, but they were arrested anyway. So was a third man who refused to leave.

4   If he had **pleaded** guilty in court, he probably would have gotten a very light punishment. Instead, he decided to **hire** a lawyer to help fight for free speech in the mall.

5   His lawyer **represents** him for free. She wants the **charge dismissed.** She says that the arrest **violated** the man's rights of free speech under the Iowa **constitution.**

6   As part of their argument, they hope to show that shopping malls are not private places. They say they are now places where people come together for social contact.

7   When malls came into the **suburbs** a few decades ago, many downtown shopping centers closed. This ended the social activities that happened there. Those social activities moved to shopping malls.

8   "Malls do more than give people a place to shop," says Professor Mills of a local university. "There are baking contests, walking clubs, flower shows and even **charity fundraisers.** They've become a new place of public gatherings."

9   Six other states, including California, Colorado, Oregon and New Jersey, say people have a right to hand out **leaflets** in malls. Last year, a judge said that that Minnesota's Mall of America, the largest mall in the U.S., is a public space. This is because millions of dollars from government programs helped build it.

10   Iowa courts will be looking closely at the Des Moines mall and at other laws. They hope to answer the question: Is a mall a public or a private place?

◆After You Read

1. Why were three young men arrested at the mall?

2. What information were they giving people?

3. Why were people upset about their arrest?

4. What is freedom of speech?

5. Why does the mall say that freedom of speech does not apply there?

6. What might have happened if the men pleaded guilty?

7. Why do some people think malls are public places?

8. What activities do people take part in at malls?

9. Do you think malls should be considered private or public places? Why?

LANGUAGE LEARNING STRATEGY

Apply the Strategy

Write summaries to help you understand your reading. When you put a reading into your own words, you understand it better. Writing a summary is a good way to check and improve your understanding of a reading.

Reread "Malls: Public Places or Private Businesses?" Then, without looking at the reading, write a short summary. Here are some instructions for writing a summary:

• Write only the main ideas, not the details.

• Leave out specific examples.

(continued on next page)

- Here is an example summary of "Shopping in Little Saigon, Texas":

Little Saigon Mall is in Haltom City, Texas. It is called Little Saigon Mall because there are many Asian shops. People go there to buy Asian food or to visit the other stores. It is a successful mall because many Vietnamese, Laotian, and Pacific Islanders live in Haltom City. The mall also attracts many non-Asian customers from the Dallas area. The mall's owner hopes that new stores will be added to the mall in the future.

- Keep your summary to one paragraph. Write it on a small index card if you have trouble keeping it short.

_____

_____

_____

_____

_____

_____

_____

Compare your summary to a partner's. What information did you leave out that your partner put in? You can make changes to your summary after you read your partner's summary.

◆Vocabulary Building

> When women are depressed, they eat or go shopping. Men invade another country. It's a whole different way of thinking.
>
> —ELAYNE BOOSLER (COMEDIAN)

Choose the correct words to fit into the blanks.

arrested	crime	hired	suburbs
charges	demonstration	leaflets	sweatshop
charity	dismissed	pleaded	violated
constitution	fundraiser	represents	

1. The three men in Iowa were _____ for handing out _____.

2. According to the _____, Americans have the right to free speech.

3. The _____ organization had a _____ to bring in money for its new programs.

4. The judge _____ the _____ against the men, and they went free.

5. It is a _____ to operate a _____, or illegal working place, in the U.S.

6. The lawyer _____ the men for free.

7. If the men had _____ guilty, they might have gotten a light punishment.

8. It _____ the mall's rules to hold a _____.

9. The area outside a city is called the _____.

10. The mall _____ security guards to protect the stores.

Test-Taking Tip

Use your journal to help you with your tests. Writing can help you in many ways on your tests. Of course, journal writing will help you practice for essay tests. But, it can help in other ways, as well. Here are some things to write about when you are thinking about tests:

- Write about your successes on tests. This will help build your confidence.

- Write down your worries about tests. Then think about whether you have good reasons for your fears. Write plans for studying.

- Write down everything you've learned in the last week. You'll surprise yourself.

◆ Getting Ready to Read   Ask three students these questions. Fill in the chart with their answers.

	Student 1	Student 2	Student 3
In your experience, have airlines provided you with good customer service?			
In your experience, have banks provided you with good customer service?			
In your experience, have department stores provided you with good customer service?			

After you get your answers, compare them with your classmates' answers. Talk about these questions:

1. Which of the three businesses gets the highest rating for customer service?

2. Which of the three businesses gets the lowest rating for customer service?

3. Do you agree with the results of the survey? Why or why not?

Vocabulary Check

Look at the words and phrases below. Put a check mark next to the ones that you know. Talk with your class about the words and phrases you don't know. Write the new words you learn in your Vocabulary Log.

_____ business class   _____ fares

_____ competitors   _____ in advance

_____ complaints   _____ monopoly

_____ customer relations   _____ premium

_____ economy   _____ productivity

_____ economy class   _____ teller

 Read   ## Reading 3: Customer Service

1 Recently, there have been a lot of **complaints** about customer service. People think customer service in the U.S. is the worst it's ever been. And, because in today's **economy** more people perform services than before, poor customer service is more common.

2 The biggest complaints are against the large airlines, banks, department stores, telephone and television cable companies. Although it seems customer service should be important in these big businesses, in fact, these companies seem less concerned than smaller businesses. Part of the problem comes when one company has too much power. This is called a **monopoly**. When a company has no **competitors**, there is no reason to provide good service.

3 Many people think the airlines in particular have had a great decrease in the quality of their customer service. **Business class** passengers, for example, now get the basic service that **economy class** passengers used to get. And it costs money. The airlines call it "**premium** service." This is true not only of the airlines, but of banks, and even of department stores.

4 Banks often charge customers for even simple services. Freida Ullrich, a bank customer says, "It costs money to use the ATM. It also costs money to use the **teller**. I think they forget that I'm the customer. They act like it's their money, not mine."

5 The companies say that part of the problem is that customers want to have it all. They want cheap prices *and* good service. So, many companies choose low prices over good service. Airline **fares** are a good example. Customers can get very good prices on the Internet or by

buying **in advance**. However, these prices mean less service. So, passengers can't expect to be served the best food and free drinks.

6   Although consumers care about price, they say service is still very important to them. Department stores with good service sell more than those that focus only on prices. And of course, some airlines and banks still care about service. They know that customer satisfaction is very important, and they want customers to return.

7   But the wrong kind of customer service is not helpful, either. Some shoppers don't like the "greeters" at the front door who say "hello" when they walk in. "The problem is," says Yung See, "they say hello, but then there's no one to help you when you shop. Why are they at the door, and not helping people in the store?"

8   The American economy also focuses on **productivity;** that is, making more with less. In a service economy, that is very difficult to do without getting bad service as a result.

9   However, companies aren't ignoring the problem. When a customer is not satisfied he or she usually tells nine people, and each of those people share that story with nine others, and so on. The smallest problem can result in a big headache for a company. Many companies hold special classes to teach their employees good **customer relations.**

10   So customer service pays, but how much?

◀ **After You Read**

1. Why is poor customer service more common today?
2. Which kinds of companies have bad reputations for customer service?
3. What is a monopoly?
4. How do monopolies affect customer service?
5. What are some examples of customer service complaints?
6. Why do some companies focus on low prices and not on service?
7. How do some companies hope to improve their service?
8. Do you have any stories about poor customer service to tell?
9. Do you have any stories about good customer service to tell?
10. Do you think customer service is getting worse or better? Why?

When you go to buy, use your eyes, not your ears.

—CZECH PROVERB

LANGUAGE LEARNING STRATEGY

Understand the difference between facts and opinions to better understand your reading. Some writers may not write the words "I think . . ." or "I believe . . ." when they are writing their opinion. It is

(continued on next page)

important to understand the difference between facts and opinions in writing. Facts are usually things you could check in other places. For example, if a writer says, "Shopping on the Internet has increased 10% this year," you can probably find that information from another source. However, if a writer says, "Shopping on the Internet is enjoyable," this is an opinion: some people might agree, and others might disagree.

When you understand the difference between fact and opinion, you do not misunderstand an author's point of view.

Apply the Strategy

Look at these statements. Then decide if they are facts or opinions. Explain your reasons. After you finish, talk them over with a partner.

_____ 1. There have been a lot of complaints about customer service.

_____ 2. Customer service is the worst it's ever been.

_____ 3. The worst companies are the airlines, the banks, large department stores, telephone and television cable companies.

_____ 4. Banks often charge customers for even simple services.

_____ 5. Banks act like it's their money, not the customers'.

_____ 6. Customers can get very good prices on the Internet or by buying in advance.

_____ 7. Many companies hold special classes to teach good customer relations.

◆ Vocabulary Building

Match the word in Column A with its meaning in Column B.

Column A	Column B
1. rival	A. fare
2. criticism	B. in advance
3. system of money and business	C. premium
4. price	D. productivity
5. efficiency	E. teller
6. before	F. competitor
7. bank clerk	G. complaint
8. best	H. economy

 **Grammar You Can Use**

Irregular Verbs

Irregular verbs are common in English. In each of the readings in this chapter, you have seen irregular verbs. It may seem that the only way to remember irregular verbs is to memorize them. In fact, some irregular verbs follow a certain pattern. Look at the chart below and fill in the blanks. If you aren't sure how to fill in one of the blanks, review the examples given.

Base Form	Simple Past Tense	Past Participle
blow	blew	blown
throw		
grow		
fly		
lend	lent	lent
bend		
send		
steal	stole	stolen
speak		
break		
wear	wore	worn
swear		
tear		
let	let	let
bet		
set		

The previous chart gives you only a few examples of irregular verbs. When you see them in your reading, it will help you to remember them if you think of other similar verbs.

Getting Ready to Read

TUNING IN: "Internet Shopping"

Before you watch the video, discuss these questions with your classmates:

© CNN

- What is the Internet?

- What is a web site?

- Have you ever used the Internet? Name a web site you have visited, and describe it for your class.

Below are some important words and phrases you will hear in the video. Which ones are related to shopping? Which ones are related to computers? Circle the words related to shopping. Underline the words related to computers. Some might apply to both.

buyers	always open	gift wrapping
web surfing	name brand products	crowds
software	incentives	ease
shoppers		

After you watch the video "Internet Shopping," answer these questions with your classmates.

1. What is RoboShopper?

2. Why don't some people like to use Internet malls?

3. What is VeriSign?

4. Would you like to shop at an Internet mall? Why or why not?

Vocabulary Check

Look at the words on the next page. Put a check mark next to the words that you know. Talk about the words you don't know with your class. Write the new words you learn in your Vocabulary Log.

> **No matter how long you shop for an item, after you've bought it, it will be on sale cheaper.**
>
> **—ANONYMOUS**

| _____ aisles | _____ obvious | _____ produce (noun) |
| _____ appeals | _____ pick out | _____ spoiled (adjective) |

Read

Reading 4: Groceries Online

1 Sharon Suarez dreams of the day when she won't have to carry groceries from her car to her house. That day has come. A growing number of people are shopping the **aisles** of grocery stores on the Internet.

2 "I've never done it, but it sounds great," Ms. Suarez said. "It is so hot here in the summer. It's also really cold in the winter. I would love to stay inside and have the groceries come to me."

3 Of course, people already buy books, do their banking, and shop for gifts on the Internet. But when they need to shop for food, most still get in the car and go to the supermarket. In fact, fewer than 1 million people have bought groceries online. The average American visits a supermarket 2.2 times a week.

4 Part of the problem is **obvious**. Many shoppers want to see the food they buy. While they might buy a CD or a book without seeing it, most people don't want to buy **produce** the same way. They also enjoy going to the supermarket. They like to walk in the aisles, and see what new items are available. Shoppers also worry about **spoiled** food, large delivery charges, and late deliveries. But, all this is slowly changing. Consumers are beginning to find that buying food online saves them time. And, they are finding that delivery is fast, cheap, and the food is good.

5 "I wasn't sure what to expect when I started ordering online, " said Michael Koklos. Mr. Koklos started shopping online when he had to work longer hours. "I never had time to shop. It is really easy and convenient to buy over the Internet. The vegetables are

better than ones I would **pick out** myself," he added. "And I never have to find a parking space."

6   While online shopping **appeals** to a certain group of the people, there will always be some who enjoy shopping for their own groceries.

7   Marti Lavalle, a shopper in a local grocery store, says she'll never shop for groceries online. "I still don't know how to use a computer," she explained.

After You Read

1. Why does Ms. Suarez like the idea of Internet grocery shopping?

2. Why is food shopping online not as popular as other types of online shopping?

3. What kinds of things do people buy on the Internet?

4. What do people think will go wrong if they buy food on the Internet?

5. Why did Mr. Koklos start food shopping online?

6. Why does he like it?

7. Would you shop for food online? Why or why not?

Vocabulary Building

Answer the questions below. Show that you understand the words in **bold**.

1. What can you find in the **produce** aisle? _____

_____

2. What about Internet shopping **appeals** to you? _____

_____

3. What is an **obvious** problem with Internet shopping? _____

_____

4. What kind of item do you like to **pick out** yourself? _____

_____

5. Why does some food **spoil**? _____

_____

PUTTING IT ALL TOGETHER

Look at the following information about two new online shopping services. With a partner, decide which service you will use. Write a summary of your decision. Explain your opinions.

	CompuFood	GrocerNet
Monthly fee:	Free	$5.95
Delivery fee:	$10 for orders under $50; free for orders over $50	Always free
Return policy:	You can return items when you get your next delivery	You can return items by calling for a pickup
Usual wait for a delivery:	One day	Two days
Price examples:	1 pound of rice: $.69 1 can of fish: $.99 Paper towels: $1.69	1 pound of rice: $.74 1 can of fish: $1.04 Paper towels: $1.69
Number of products:	20,000	30,000
Customer service:	Phone line open 24 hours a day, 7 days a week. $1 per phone call.	Phone line open from 8 a.m. to midnight, 6 days a week (closed Sunday). A free call.

CHECK YOUR PROGRESS

On a scale of 1 to 5, rate how well you've mastered the goals set at the beginning of the chapter:

1 2 3 4 5   write summaries to help you understand your reading.

1 2 3 4 5   understand the difference between fact and opinion.

1 2 3 4 5   plan enough time to complete assignments.

1 2 3 4 5   use your journal to help with tests.

1 2 3 4 5   remember irregular verb forms.

If you've given yourself a 3 or lower on any of these goals:

- visit the *Tapestry* web site for additional practice.
- ask your instructor for extra help.
- review the sections of the chapter that you found difficult.
- work with a partner or study group to further your progress.

Look at this photo of a satellite that can receive radio signals from space. Then discuss these questions with your classmates:

- Do you enjoy learning about space?
- Do you think there is life on other planets?
- Do you think that in the future we will we be able to communicate with life on other planets?

SPACE IS THE PLACE

This chapter contains information about space: the planets, the sun, and the stars, and the people who travel through space. The readings in this chapter talk about both what we know and what we don't know about space.

Setting Goals

In this chapter, you will learn how to:

◈ make outlines of readings.

◈ understand and use acronyms.

◈ find and use campus resources.

◈ understand comparative forms.

◈ celebrate your success on tests.

Which goal is most important to you? _____

_____

Why? _____

Talk about your answers with your class.

◆ **Getting Started**

1. Before you start reading about space, look through this chapter quickly. Which title looks most interesting?

   _____

2. Which readings do you already know something about?

   _____

   _____

3. The readings in this chapter have many acronyms. On what page in this chapter can you find a discussion about acronyms?

   _____

◆ **Getting Ready to Read**

What do you already know about astronauts? Brainstorm your background knowledge about astronauts, and write the words, phrases, and ideas you think of in the box.

```
                        Astronauts




```

> **That's one small step for man; one giant leap for mankind.**
>
> **—NEIL ARMSTRONG, FIRST WORDS SPOKEN BY A MAN WALKING ON THE MOON, 20 JULY 1969**

Vocabulary Check

Look at the words below. Put a check mark next to the words that you know. Talk with your class about the ones you don't know. Write the new words you learn in your Vocabulary Log.

_____ bulky	_____ fit	_____ simulators
_____ crew	_____ launching	_____ space shuttle
_____ denser	_____ maneuvering	_____ space suits
_____ eager	_____ orbit	_____ trains (verb)
_____ equipped	_____ pressure	_____ voyage
_____ extreme	_____ selects	_____ weightless

LANGUAGE LEARNING STRATEGY

Learn how to understand and use acronyms to help you remember information. Acronyms are initials that are used instead of a full phrase. Each initial of the acronym stands for the first letter of one of the words that you are trying to remember. For example, many American students, when learning about the Great Lakes, remember the word "homes."

Huron   Ontario   Michigan   Erie   Superior

These are the names of the five Great Lakes.

Acronyms are used to shorten longer phrases. For example, SCUBA is a famous acronym for the phrase "self-contained underwater breathing apparatus." NASA is an acronym for the National Aeronautics and Space Administration.

Apply the Strategy

1. Look through the readings in this chapter and find some acronyms. Write down two acronyms on the lines on the left. Next to each acronym write what it stands for.

   _____   _____

   _____   _____

2. Think of an acronym that you can use to remember something important. You can make your acronym using your first language or English. Share your acronym with the class.

 Read

Reading 1: All About Astronauts

1　In the United States, the NASA Space Program **selects** and **trains** new astronauts every two years. Of all the **eager** men and women that apply, only about twenty are chosen. The future astronauts must be physically **fit** and have a good education, as well as have the ability to work well with others.

2　*Training:* An astronaut begins his or her training at the Johnson Space Center in Houston, Texas. At the Space Center, they learn to perform all the tasks that will be required of them while in space. They also learn what to do in emergency situations.

Astronauts in training perform these tasks and emergency drills for several months until they are ready for new challenges.

3   While in training, the astronauts also learn about the equipment they will be using in space. Flight **simulators** are used to practice safely **launching,** navigating, and landing the **space shuttle.** Also, the astronauts test out the **bulky space suits** they will need to wear if they ever walk in space. Believe it or not, the swimming pool is the place that astronauts train with their heavy space suits. Because water is **denser** and more supportive than air, it is a good way to get used to the **weightless** feeling of being in **orbit.**

4   *Liftoff, Orbit, and Spacewalks:* Astronauts wear different clothes during launch and re-entry to Earth than they do during the rest of their **voyage.** This special suit, which includes a helmet, gloves, and boots, protects them from the changes in **pressure** and temperature as the shuttle leaves or comes back to the Earth. Once in orbit, the astronauts are free to wear whatever they find most comfortable.

5   To walk outside the shuttle, astronauts need yet another suit, called an "extravehicular[1] **maneuvering** unit" or EMU. In this suit, the astronaut can talk to the **crew** aboard the shuttle, and is protected from the **extreme** temperatures of space. The EMU is also **equipped** with drinking water and oxygenated air.[2]

Source: http:ispec.scibernet.com/station/

After You Read

1. How often does NASA select new astronauts?

2. About how many new astronauts are chosen?

3. Where do astronauts get training?

4. What do astronauts learn during training?

5. Why do astronauts train in swimming pools?

6. What kinds of clothing do astronauts wear during a launch?

[1]*Extravehicular* means "outside the vehicle."

[2]*Oxygenated air* is air with extra oxygen added.

7. What is an EMU?

8. The reading "All About Astronauts" gives three qualities an astronaut should have. Write the three qualities here:

a. _____

b. _____

c. _____

What other qualities do you think an astronaut should have? Discuss this with a partner. Write some other qualities here:

1. _____

2. _____

3. _____

4. _____

Share your ideas with your class.

 **Vocabulary Building**

This reading contains many new nouns and adjectives. Choose one noun and one adjective from each column, then write a sentence using them. Do this until all the words are used up. One is done for you as an example.

ADJECTIVES	NOUNS	Sentence
bulky	~~crew~~	1. The crew was very physically fit.
dense	launch	2.
eager	orbit	3.
equipped	pressure	4.
extreme	shuttle	5.
~~fit~~	space suit	6.
weightless	voyage	7.

LANGUAGE LEARNING STRATEGY

Make an outline to find the most important information in a reading. To make an outline, list the main idea from a topic sentence first (review the strategy on topic sentences on page 72). Then list the ideas which support the topic sentence. You do not have to write the whole sentence. You should only write the idea from each sentence. For example, an outline of the first paragraph of "All About Astronauts" could start like this:

I. NASA selects and trains astronauts   (topic sentence idea)
   every two years.

   A. only 20 chosen   (supporting idea)

   B. must be physically fit   (supporting idea)

   C. must have a good education   (supporting idea)

   D. must work well with others   (supporting idea)

Writing an outline helps you understand the organization and the content of a reading.

Apply the Strategy

Complete the outline below using the information from the reading "All About Astronauts."

I. NASA selects and trains astronauts every two years.

   A. only 20 chosen

   B. must be physically fit

   C. must have a good education

   D. must work well with others

II. _____

   A. perform tasks required in space

   B. _____

   C. practice for several months

III. Training equipment

   A. _____

   B. _____

   C. train in the swimming pool

IV. Clothing worn at launch/in orbit

   A. _____

   B. _____

V. _____

   A. can talk to crew

   B. protected from extreme temperatures

   C. _____

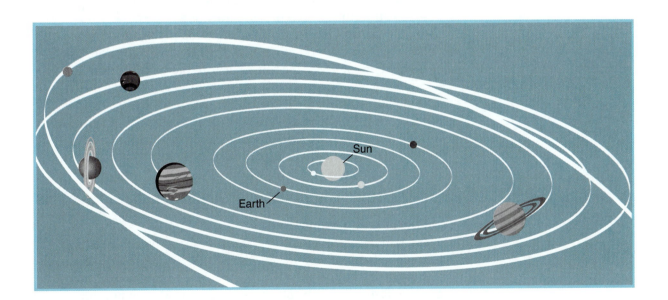

◆ Getting Ready to Read   Look at the picture of our solar system. Then, in groups, discuss these questions:

1. What are the names of the planets in our solar system (in your native language)?

2. Do you know the English names of these planets?

3. Compare your information with the rest of your classmates.

> The astronomer Edwin Hubble (1889–1953) discovered that the galaxies in the universe are moving farther and farther apart.

Vocabulary Check

Look at the words below. Put a check mark next to the words you know. Talk with your class about the words you don't know. Write the new words you learn in your Vocabulary Log.

_____ astronomers	_____ crushing	_____ solar system
_____ circling	_____ galaxy	_____ telescopes
_____ constellation	_____ gravity	_____ wobbling
_____ cosmic	_____ hospitable	

 Read

Reading 2: Found: A New Solar System

1 **Astronomers** have never liked the idea that our **solar system**—the sun and its family of nine planets—is the only one in the **galaxy.** They just couldn't imagine how one star could have planets and the other billions of stars have none.

2 So scientists have been searching through their **telescopes** for years, trying to find some evidence that other planets are **circling** around stars like the sun. Finally, they found a new planet.

3 The newly discovered planet is orbiting a star called 51 Pegasus in the **constellation** named for the winged horse of Greek mythology. It is about 40 light-years, or a bit more than 235 trillion miles, from Earth—pretty close in **cosmic** terms.

4 The discovery was first announced by Swiss astronomers. It took a second sighting by Americans at Lick Observatory near San Jose, California, before scientists were convinced. They didn't actually see the planet, but they saw 51 Pegasus **wobbling** as the planet's **gravity** tugged on it.

5 Is there life on this distant planet? Probably not. Its huge size means it has **crushing** gravity. Also, it orbits so close to its parent star that the temperature is hotter than the hottest oven.

6 Still, there could be other planets circling 51 Pegasus, and maybe some are more **hospitable** to life. And who knows how many other stars have their own solar systems?

An Unearthly World

7 Not much is known about the new planet, but here are some ways it differs from our own.

	Earth	New Planet
Distance from its sun	93 million miles	5 million miles
Size	6.6 sextillion tons (6,600,000,000,000,000,000,000)	160 times bigger than Earth
Average surface temperature	57 degrees F	1800 degrees F
Length of a year (the time it takes to orbit its sun)	365 days	4 days
Is life possible?	Yes	Not likely

Source: *Time for Kids,* September 27, 1995, Vol. 1, #6

◀ After You Read

The three brightest objects in the solar system are the Sun, the Moon, and Venus.

1. Where is the new planet?

2. What star is it orbiting?

3. Who first discovered the new planet?

4. Did the scientists see the planet?

5. How do they know the planet is there?

6. Do you think there could there be life on this planet? Why or Why not?

◀ Vocabulary Building

Choose the correct word to fill in the blanks.

astronomers	cosmic	gravity
circling	crushing	solar system
constellation	galaxy	telescopes

1. _____ use _____ to look at the stars.

2. The _____ on Pegasus 51 would be _____ because of its size.

3. _____ is another name for orbiting.

4. A _____ is a group of stars that usually have a name.

5. _____ is a word related to all the universe.

6. A _____ is another name for a _____.

◆**Grammar You Can Use**

Comparative Forms

Use the comparative form of an adjective to compare two things. One way to make a comparative is to add *-er* to one-syllable adjectives:

fast → faster

Use the word "than" after the comparative adjective in a sentence:

A space shuttle is *faster than* an airplane.

Now try to write your own sentences using information about the two planets in the chart "An Unearthly World":

1. Earth / New Planet   close   to its sun

   _____

   _____

   _____

2. Earth / New Planet   small

   _____

   _____

   _____

3. Earth / New Planet   cold

   _____

   _____

   _____

4. Earth / New Planet   short   year

   _____

   _____

   _____

◆**Getting Ready to Read**

Look at the photo on the next page and discuss these questions with your classmates:

- What is a comet?

- Have you ever seen a comet? Where and when?

- What do you know about comets?

Vocabulary Check

Look at the words below. Put a check mark next to the ones that you know. Talk with your class about the words you don't know. Write the new words you learn in your Vocabulary Log.

_____ appreciation   _____ dinosaurs   _____ primitive

_____ asteroid   _____ emperor   _____ reflects

_____ binoculars   _____ horizon   _____ snowballs

_____ comet   _____ left over   _____ tidal waves

_____ diameter   _____ origins   _____ wipe out

Comet Halley was first seen in 240 BCE. The next sighting will be in 2061.

◆ Read

Reading 3: Hale-Bopp

1 Just above the **horizon,** a ball of light left a trail of stardust[1] in the evening sky. **Comet** Hale-Bopp, brighter than most of the stars, was a beautiful sight. It was 1997, and people had not seen this comet for 4,210 years.

2 Comet Hale-Bopp, one of the brightest comets of this century, brought crowds to telescopes and **binoculars.** It also brought people out to their back yards, parks, and roofs. If only for a few weeks, the comet put excitement back into the night sky for people of the modern world.

3 "I saw it for the first time last night. I got so excited I made my son come into the back yard to see it," said Felix Nash of Springfield. "This comet really is amazing."

4 Comets are made of dust, rock, and ice. These "space **snowballs**" float in the solar

[1]Stardust is the pieces of stars left in the sky.

system away from the sun. Sometimes gravity from a star pushes a comet towards earth, but we really only see a few comets from earth. At the edge of the solar system, there is a place called the Oort Cloud. Scientists think there could be more than 100 billion comets in the Oort cloud.

5   Scientists don't really know how comets started, but they have two theories. Some think that they were formed when the solar system began billions of years ago. They think comets are **left over** rock, dust, and ice. Others think that comets were pulled together by the sun's gravity a long time ago.

6   Hale-Bopp was the most watched comet since the 1910 appearance of Halley's Comet. Hale-Bopp, in fact, was one of the 32 great comets of the past 1,000 years, according to astronomers.

7   Throughout history, human beings have viewed comets with fear. They thought they were signs of the gods' anger. One comet caused the ancient Roman **emperor** Nero to murder his mother, brother, and two wives. In 1910, Halley's Comet terrified millions of people as newspapers said that it might **wipe out** life on Earth.

8   In modern times, people watched Hale-Bopp with simple **appreciation.** "You can look up at this comet and wonder what Nero thought, or what **primitive** people thought thousands of years ago," said Frank Thompson, an astronomer. "Today, we can just watch the beauty."

9   When you see a comet, you're seeing more than a temporary light show. You're also seeing a bit of the **origins** of our solar system and, perhaps, of life itself. You also may be looking at a cosmic relative of a comet that may have hit the Earth 65 million years ago. Many astronomers think such a comet may have set the world's forests on fire, caused **tidal waves,** darkened the skies, and killed off the **dinosaurs.** Scientists now generally agree that a disaster like this occurred, although they aren't sure whether it was a comet or an **asteroid.** Asteroids are pieces of rock or metal that come from a different part of the solar system.

10   Hale-Bopp was so bright because of its size. Astronomers estimate it had a 25-mile **diameter**—about 10 times larger than the average comet. The bigger the dirty snowball, the more light it **reflects.** No comet in recorded history has been that bright. In ancient times, such brightness frightened people. We are fortunate today that we can just watch.

After You Read

1. What is a comet?

2. What is important about Hale-Bopp?

3. Before 1997, when was the last time it was seen?

4. What are comets made of?

5. How did people behave when they saw comets in the past?

6. What is the Oort Cloud?

7. Where do comets come from?

8. What do some astronomers think happened as a result of a comet hitting the earth 65 million years ago?

9. How big was Hale-Bopp?

10. Why was Hale-Bopp so bright?

◈ Vocabulary Building

Use these words to answer the questions:

asteroids	horizon
binoculars	reflects
comets	solar systems
dinosaurs	telescopes
emperor	tidal waves

1. These things are found in space: _____ , _____ and _____

3. These can be used to look into space: _____ and _____

4. These were once found on earth: _____

5. The moon _____ the sun's light.

6. These happen in the oceans: _____

7. Nero was one of these: _____

8. This is what you see when you look out over the landscape: the _____

ACADEMIC POWER STRATEGY

Apply the Strategy

Find and use campus resources when you need help with your classes. Campus resources include libraries, tutorial centers, and computer labs. All of these places have people who can help you with specific problems. Knowing where to find resources will help you become more successful in your studies.

1. Look at a campus map, read your college schedule, or go to your student resource center to locate your campus resources.

2. Find out when the resource is available and if you need an appointment.

3. Think of the problem you need help with. Write down specific questions to ask at the campus resource before you go.

4. Report to your class or what you learned.

Test-Taking Tip

Celebrate your success on tests to keep your motivation high. When you don't do well on a test, you probably punish yourself by going over and over every mistake in your head. What do you do when you succeed, even if it's a small success?

Celebrating your success is important. You will get motivation for future tests, and feel less worried about future tests. So, after a successful test, treat yourself by going for a special meal, by getting together with friends for a relaxing evening, or by doing something else you enjoy.

◆ **Getting Ready to Read**

Before you read "SETI: Search for Extraterrestrial Intelligence," talk about these questions with your class:

- What would happen if we found life on another planet?
- What do you think life from another planet might look like?

Vocabulary Check

Look at the words below. Put a check mark next to the ones that you know. Talk with your class about the words you don't know. Write the new words you learn in your Vocabulary Log.

_____ broadcast	_____ investigates	_____ signals
_____ detected	_____ microwave	_____ verified
_____ evolution	_____ observatory	
_____ extraterrestrial	_____ planetary	

◆ **Read**

Reading 4: SETI: Search for Extraterrestrial Intelligence

1 SETI is an acronym for "Search for Extraterrestrial Intelligence." SETI is a scientific organization that **investigates** life on other planets in our galaxy and outside our solar system. SETI also has projects in other fields such as astronomy, **planetary** sciences, and **evolution.** Many scientists, engineers, administrators, technicians, and teachers work at SETI.

2 Project Phoenix is the name of SETI's main research project. This project searches for **extraterrestrial** intelligence. Project Phoenix uses the world's most sophisticated equipment to look in outer space. They look especially for **signals** on the **microwave** band from 1,000 MHz (Megahertz) to 3,000 MHz. This microwave band contains a narrow **"broadcast"** band. Extraterrestrial (ET) researchers think that this is the band that life on other planets would use for communication.

3 Project Phoenix has not **detected** any ET signals yet. If an unusual signal is found, the scientists must be able to show that it came

from outside our solar system. In 1977, an unusual signal was found at the Ohio State Radio **Observatory.** Unfortunately, the signal could not be **verified** by scientists. The signal was never heard again. Nothing like this has ever happened at SETI. But what if SETI discovered a signal? Would they reply to the signal? Right now, SETI does not plan to reply to any signals

they find. If they found a signal, the nations of the Earth would have to decide whether or not to reply. This means the senders of the signal may never know the Earth received their signal. Also, it might take decades to send signals back. The receivers would be very far away, and it would take light-years[1] for the signals to travel to them.

After You Read

Write the answers to these questions. Use complete sentences in your answers.

1. What is SETI?
2. What does SETI do?
3. Who works at SETI?
4. What is SETI's main research project?
5. Have there ever been any unusual signals? Where and when?
6. What would happen if SETI found an ET signal?
7. What problems are there with sending and receiving SETI signals?
8. Do you think any unusual signals will be found? Why or why not?

> Jupiter weighs twice as much as all the other planets combined.

Vocabulary Building

The vocabulary in this reading may seem difficult. But, if you look closely at the words, you will probably realize that you know many words related to them, or that have the same parts. Cross out the word in each row that does not share the same parts as the word in **bold**. Underline the parts of the word that are the same. Finally, match the underlined part to its meanings (write the letter in the blank). The first is done for you as an example.

Meaning

_E_ 1. <u>detect</u>ed	<u>detect</u>ive	~~contact~~	A. earth
___ 2. evolution	evaluate	evolve	B. large body in space
___ 3. extraterrestrial	terrain	terminal	C. look into
___ 4. investigate	request	investigator	D. see
___ 5. microwave	macaroni	microcomputer	E. find out
___ 6. observatory	receive	observe	F. truth
___ 7. planetary	planets	explain	G. change
___ 8. verified	conserve	verification	H. very small

[1]A light-year is 5.875×10^{12} miles

TUNING IN: "The CIA and UFOs"

© CNN

Sometimes, people see something in the sky that they cannot explain. The things they see are called UFOs or Unidentified Flying Objects. Often, people think that UFOs are really space ships from another planet. In this video, you will learn about the United States Air Force investigation of UFOs. The Air Force investigation was called "Operation Blue Book." In a report about "Operation Blue Book," the Air Force said that there were no UFOs. They said that people saw weather balloons or lights in the sky. Now, the Central Intelligence Agency (CIA), a part of the U.S. government, has written a new report. The CIA says that the Air Force lied about the UFOs.

Put a check mark next to the words and phrases you know. Discuss with your class the words and phrases you don't know. Write new words you learn in your Vocabulary Log.

_____ high altitude   _____ misleading

_____ deceptive   _____ flying saucer

_____ conspiracy   _____ flares

_____ cover up   _____ aliens

_____ Cold War   _____ dummies

Watch the video. Fill out this information as you watch.

> "This led the _____ to make misleading and
>
> _____ statements to the _____ in order
>
> to ally public fears and to protect an extraordinarily sensitive
>
> _____ security project."
>
> "While perhaps justified, this _____ added fuel
>
> to the later _____ theories and the _____
>
> controversy of the late 1970s."

Read the questions below and discuss the answers with your class.

1. According to the CIA, why did the Air Force lie about the UFOs?

2. What were the "UFOs"?

3. What happened in Roswell, New Mexico, according to the Air Force?

4. Do you think the Air Force is telling the truth now? Do you think there are UFOs?

PUTTING IT ALL TOGETHER
• •

In this chapter, you learned how to find and use campus resources. You also learned how to outline a reading. In this activity, you will practice these strategies.

1. Go to your campus library or the Internet and find a short article about one of these topics:

   UFOs   The Universe

   Astronauts   SETI

   Comets   The Universe

2. Read your article carefully. Write an outline for your article.

3. Bring your article and your outline to class. Share the information from your article with your classmates.

CHECK YOUR PROGRESS
• •

On a scale of 1 to 5, rate how well you've mastered the goals set at the beginning of the chapter:

1 2 3 4 5   make outlines of readings.

1 2 3 4 5   understand and use acronyms.

1 2 3 4 5   find and use campus resources.

1 2 3 4 5   understand comparative forms.

1 2 3 4 5   celebrate your success on a test.

If you've given yourself a 3 or lower on any of these goals:

• visit the *Tapestry* web site for additional practice.

• ask your instructor for extra help.

• review the sections of the chapter that you found difficult.

• work with a partner or study group to further your progress.

SKILLS INDEX

TEXT CREDITS

Pages 13–14: "The College Classroom," Lynda Corbin, *City Times,* December 1993. Reprinted with permission.

Pages 48–49: "Caffeine" from *The Drug Alert Dictionary and Resource Guide,* by Jeffrey Shulman.

Pages 146–147: "Awasassi: An Ojibwe Folktale," Lois Beardslee, *Cobblestone,* November 1998. Reprinted with permission.

Pages 179–180: "All About Astronauts," http://www.ispec-webmaster@scibernet.com.

Pages 184–185: "Found: A New Solar System," from *Time For Kids,* September 27, 1995. Reprinted with permission.

PHOTO CREDITS

pp. 2, 18, 24, Photographs by Jonathan Stark for the Heinle & Heinle Image Resource Bank; p. 32, Amy C. Erta/PhotoEdit; p. 37, Corbis/Michael S. Yamashita; pp. 40, 42, T Photographs by Jonathan Stark for the Heinle & Heinle Image Resource Bank; p. 42, B Corbis/Kevin R. Morris; p. 45, Corbis/Mike King; p. 60, L Corbis/Michael S. Yamashita; p. 60, M Corbis/Tecmap Corporation; p. 60, R Corbis/Kevin Shafer; p. 64, Corbis/Dave G. Houser; p. 68, L Corbis/Joe McDonald; L C & C Corbis/D. Robert Franz, R C Corbis/Gunter Marx, R Corbis/Joe McDonald; p. 70, T L Corbis/Alissa Crandall, T R Corbis/Tom Brakefield, B Corbis/Danny Lehman; pp. 80, 83, Photographs by Jonathan Stark for the Heinle & Heinle Image Resource Bank; p. 87, Corbis/Craig Lovell; p. 92, Corbis/Bettmann; p. 96, Corbis/Bettmann; p. 100, Corbis/Trisha Rafferty, Eye Ubiquitous; p. 108, Corbis/Bettmann; p. 113, Corbis/Bojan Brecel; p. 120, T Corbis/Robert van der Hilst, B Provided by editorial, p. 129, T L, B L & R Photographs by Jonathan Stark for the Heinle & Heinle Image Resource Bank; p. 129, T M Corbis/Bettmann; p. 136, Corbis/Lyn Hughes; p. 140, Corbis/Bettmann; p. 146, Corbis/Larson Wood; p. 149, Corbis/Kevin R. Morris; p. 159, Photograph by Jonathan Stark for the Heinle & Heinle Image Resource Bank; p. 161, Corbis/Nevada Weir; pp. 164, 173, 176, Photographs by Jonathan Stark for the Heinle & Heinle Image Resource Bank; p. 180, Corbis/Roger Ressmeyer; p. 187, Corbis/Aaron Horowitz